Studies in modern capitalism · Etudes sur le capitalisme moderne

Algeria 1960

Studies in modern capitalism · Etudes sur le capitalisme moderne

Editorial board · Comité de rédaction
Maurice Aymard, Maison des Sciences de l'Homme, Paris
Jacques Revel, Ecole des Hautes Etudes en Sciences Sociales, Paris
Immanuel Wallerstein, Fernand Braudel Center for the Study of Economies, Historical Systems, and Civilizations, Binghamton, New York

This series is devoted to an attempt to comprehend capitalism as a world-system. It will include monographs, collections of essays and colloquia around specific themes, written by historians and social scientists united by a common concern for the study of large-scale, long-term social structure and social change.

The series is a joint enterprise of the Maison des Sciences de l'Homme in Paris and the Fernand Braudel Center for the Study of Economies, Historical Systems, and Civilizations at the State University of New York at Binghamton.

Other books in the series
Immanuel Wallerstein: *The capitalist world-economy*
Andre Gunder Frank: *Mexican agriculture 1521–1630: transformation of the mode of production*

This book is published as part of the joint publishing agreement established in 1977 between the Fondation de la Maison des Sciences de l'Homme and the Syndics of the Cambridge University Press. Titles published under this arrangement may appear in any European language or, in the case of volumes of collected essays, in several languages.

New books will appear either as individual titles or in one of the series which the Maison des Sciences de l'Homme and the Cambridge University Press have jointly agreed to publish. All books published jointly by the Maison des Sciences de l'Homme and the Cambridge University Press will be distributed by the Press throughout the world.

Algeria 1960

The disenchantment of the world
The sense of honour
The Kabyle house or the world reversed

Essays by
PIERRE BOURDIEU
Directeur d'études
Ecole des Hautes Etudes en Sciences Sociales

Translated by Richard Nice

Cambridge University Press
Cambridge   London   New York   Melbourne

& Editions de la Maison des Sciences de l'Homme
Paris

Published by the Syndics of the Cambridge University Press
The Pitt Building, Trumpington Street, Cambridge CB2 1RP
Bentley House, 200 Euston Road, London NW1 2DB
32 East 57th Street, New York, NY 10022, USA
296 Beaconsfield Parade, Middle Park, Melbourne 3206, Australia
and Editions de la Maison des Sciences de l'Homme
54 Boulevard Raspail, 75270 Paris Cedex 06

Original French version of "Algeria 1960" © Editions de Minuit 1963
Original French version of "The sense of honour" and "The Kabyle house"
© Pierre Bourdieu 1972

English translation © Maison des Sciences de l'Homme and
Cambridge University Press 1979

English translation first published 1979

Printed in Great Britain at the University Press, Cambridge

Library of Congress Cataloguing in Publication Data
Bourdieu, Pierre.
Algeria 1960.
(Studies in modern capitalism)
Translation of Algérie 60.
Includes index.
1. Algeria – Economic conditions. 2. Economic development – Case studies.
3. Capitalism – Case studies. I. Title. II. Series.
HC547.A4B6413   330.9'65'05   78-4237
ISBN 0 521 22090 4

Contents

Preface	*page* vii
The disenchantment of the world	1
Introduction	1
1 Simple reproduction and cyclical time	8
2 Contradictory necessities and ambiguous conduct	30
3 Subjective hopes and objective chances	50
4 The economic conditions for transformed economic dispositions	64
Conclusion	92
The sense of honour	95
The Kabyle house or the world reversed	133
Index	155

Preface

The present text of my first essay, written in 1963 for a foreign-language edition, is a shortened version of *Travail et travailleurs en Algérie* (published in 1963), which presented the findings of a series of ethnographic and statistical studies carried out in Algeria between 1958 and 1961.¹

It was not by chance that the relationship between structures and habitus² was constituted as a theoretical problem in relation to a historical situation in which that problem was in a sense presented by reality itself, in the form of a permanent *discrepancy* between the agents' economic dispositions and the economic world in which they had to act. In situations of transition between a pre-capitalist economy and a capitalist economy, the objectivist abstraction in which neo-marginalists join hands with structural-Marxists is so flagrantly inadequate that one has to be blind to reality to reduce the economic agents to mere reflections of the economic structures and to fail to pose the problem of the genesis of economic dispositions and of the economic and social conditions of their genesis. A particular class of material conditions of existence, grasped objectively in the form of a particular structure of objective probabilities – an *objective future* – generates determinate dispositions towards the future. These dispositions are structured structures which function as structuring structures, orienting and organizing the economic practices of daily life – purchases, saving,

1. The apparatus of supporting material – statistical tables, extracts from interviews, documents, etc. – is not reprinted here. The reader should therefore consult *Travail et travailleurs en Algérie* (Paris and The Hague: Mouton, 1963) for this information; also for details of the survey methodology (sampling, questionnaire, etc.) and analysis of the findings. "The Disenchantment of the World" was published in French under the title *Algérie 60* (Paris: Editions de Minuit, 1978).
2. The habitus is a system of durable, transposable dispositions which functions as the generative basis of structured, objectively unified practices.

and credit – and also political representations, whether resigned or revolutionary. Those who have no future before them, as the phrase goes, are unlikely to form the individual project of bringing about their future, or to work for the coming of a new collective future. The relation to a future objectively inscribed in the material conditions of existence contains the basis of the distinction between the sub-proletariat and the proletariat – between the uprooted, demoralized masses' disposition to revolt and the revolutionary dispositions of organized workers who have sufficient control over their present to undertake to reappropriate the future.

Rereading this text, written more than a decade ago, I more than once felt the wish to refine and systematize the analyses, by investing in them all that subsequent work has yielded (particularly *Outline of a Theory of Practice*).[3] But, conscious of the futility of all forms of "theoretical labour" that are not accompanied by empirical work on the things themselves (which would mean, in this case, a return to fieldwork which is not possible at present), I have refrained from doing so. I have added two further essays, "The Sense of Honour" and "The Kabyle House or the World Reversed", previously available in English but in an unsatisfactory form; though they belong more closely to the line of anthropological research presented in the *Outline*, they should help to give the reader a clearer idea of the cultural presuppositions of the logic of the Kabyle economy.

P.B.

Paris
December 1976

---

3. See P. Bourdieu, *Esquisse d'une théorie de la pratique* (Geneva and Paris: Droz, 1972) (*Outline of a Theory of Practice*, Cambridge: Cambridge University Press, 1977; *Entwurf einer Theorie der Praxis*, Frankfurt: Suhrkamp, 1976).

The disenchantment of the world

For nothing is more certain, than that despair has almost the same effect on us with enjoyment, and that we are no sooner acquainted with the impossibility of satisfying any desire, than the desire itself vanishes.
David Hume, Introduction to *A Treatise of Human Nature*

Introduction

Those who pose the ritual question of the cultural obstacles to economic development are generally concerned exclusively, that is to say abstractly, with the "rationalization" of economic conducts, and they describe as resistances, solely imputable to the cultural heritage (or, worse, to one or another of its aspects, Islam for example), every failure to meet the requirements of an abstract model of "rationality" as defined by economic theory. Paradoxically, the philosophy of economic development which reduces anthropology to a dimension of economics leads to the ignoring of the *economic conditions* for the adoption of "rational" economic behaviour and expects the man of pre-capitalist societies to start by converting himself into a "developed" man in order to be able to enjoy the economic advantages of a "developed" economy.

Nor does cultural anthropology escape abstraction when it sees a simple effect of "culture contact" in the transformations of pre-capitalist societies which it describes as "culture change" or "acculturation". It tends to ignore the fact that transformation of the system of cultural models and values is not the result of a simple logical combination between the imported models and the original models but that, being both the consequence and the precondition of economic transformations, this transformation takes place only through the mediation of the experience and practice of individuals differently situated with respect to the economic system. Thus, within the apparently most homogeneous peasant society, statistical analysis reveals differences in economic dispositions which can be related to differences in economic conditions.[1] The cash economy and the system of dispositions that is linked to it develop at varying speeds in the different social classes, depending on their type of activity and especially on the intensity and duration of their previous contacts with the cash economy and, on the rebound, these inequalities in rhythm tend to widen the cleavages between the groups.[2] This single example is sufficient to recall a truth too often ignored by economists and anthropologists: inequalities in relation to the "rational" economy and economic rationality, or, to put it another way, unequal rhythms (between one individual or group and another) in the transformation of economic attitudes are primarily the reflection of economic and social inequalities.

It follows from this that the logic of the transformation of practices takes different forms depending on the economic and social situations in which it takes place. Economic practice (which one can always measure abstractly on a scale of degrees of economic "rationality") always refers back to a class condition: the subject of economic acts is not *homo economicus* but the real man, who is made by the economy. In consequence, given that the practices (both economic and non-economic) of each agent have as their common root the relation he objectively maintains, through the mediation of his habitus which is itself the product of a definite type of economic condition, with the objective and collective future which defines his class situation, only a sociology of temporal dispositions enables us to get beyond the traditional question as to whether transformation of the conditions of existence precedes and governs the transformation of dispositions or the contrary, and to determine how class condition is able to structure the whole experience of social subjects, not least their economic experience, without acting through the intermediary of mechanical determinations or of an adequate and explicit awareness of the objective truth of the situation.

1. See P. Bourdieu and A. Sayad, *Le déracinement: la crise de l'agriculture traditionelle en Algérie* (Paris: Editions de Minuit, 1964).
2. If anthropologists so rarely resort to the statistical method, this is not only because their training and the tradition of their discipline do not encourage them to use this unfamiliar technique even when it would seem to be essential, as in the study of culture changes, but also, it would appear, because they almost always think in terms of the "model" and the "rule".

The economic system imported by colonization – the objectified heritage of another civilization, a legacy of accumulated experiences, techniques of payment or marketing, methods of accountancy, calculation, and organization – has the necessity of a "cosmos" (as Weber puts it) into which the workers find themselves cast and whose rules they must learn in order to survive. Consequently, in most Third World countries, in spite of all the analogies, the situation is quite different from that of nascent capitalism. Sombart wrote that "in the early capitalist age, the entrepreneur produced capitalism, in the perfected capitalist age capitalism produces the entrepreneur".[3] And he himself went on to qualify that illuminating but oversimplifying formula: "In the young days of capitalism, capitalist organization was by no means general; it was mostly the creation of the non-capitalist genius. Its stock of knowledge and experience was not large; both experience and knowledge had to be gained, garnered, and tested. It had little in the way of capitalist machinery, and that little had to be painfully acquired. And as for the primary foundations of all contracts and agreements, they had not yet been laid; long and strenuous was the upward striving of credit and confidence and trust. Does it not stand to sense that under such circumstances the capitalist entrepreneur was bound to act on his own initiative, and possibly with a good deal of caprice?"[4] If initiative and caprice had such an important part to play, the reason is that, as Sombart indicates, the formation of what he calls the "economic outlook" and the constitution of the economic system were accomplished concurrently, because they were linked in a dialectical relation of mutual dependence and priority.

The essence of the situation of economic dependence (of which the colonial situation is the extreme case) is, by contrast, that economic and social organization is the product not of an autonomous evolution of the society transforming itself in accordance with its internal logic, but of exogenous, accelerated change, imposed by the imperialist power. In these circumstances, the extent of the free decision and initiative left to the economic agents seems to be reduced to zero; and one might think that, unlike their counterparts in the early days of capitalism, they have no option

3. W. Sombart, *The Quintessence of Capitalism: A Study of the History and Psychology of the Modern Business Man*, trans. M. Epstein (London: Unwin, 1915), p. 197 (modified).
4. *Loc. cit.*

but to adapt to the imported system. In reality, agents brought up in a quite different cultural tradition can only succeed in adapting to the cash economy by means of a creative reinvention which is the very opposite of a purely mechanical and passive forced accommodation. In this respect they are closer to the early entrepreneur than to the economic agents of capitalist societies. As it evolves, economic organization tends to impose itself as a quasi-autonomous system which expects and demands of the individual a certain type of economic practice and dispositions. The spirit of calculation and forecasting, insensibly acquired and assimilated through implicit and explicit education, thus tends to be taken for granted because "rationalization" is the atmosphere one lives and moves in.

> The material techniques required for economic conduct in the capitalist system are, as has often been shown, inseparable from a "lived philosophy" which has been built up slowly over the course of history and is transmitted both through the early education performed by the family and through formal education. As Sombart puts it, "As the demand for economic rationalism arose it was satisfied by specialist work. Thousands of people are engaged today in thinking out and carrying through the best methods of conducting business. There is a whole hierarchy of them, from the professors of economics to the army of accountants, makers of calculating machines, card-index systems, typewriters and what not. In many cases, too, the employees of business houses are urged by promises of bonuses to take part in this production of economic rationalism."[5] One "ideal–typical" anecdote (reported by the newspapers on 25 October 1959) will suffice to demonstrate how, even in childhood, the economy tends to mould the economic habitus: the public schoolboys of Lowestoft (England) set up an insurance society. For a beating a boy who was insured received four shillings. But because the system was being abused, the chairman, aged thirteen, had to insist on a supplementary clause whereby the society was not liable for "accidents" deliberately incurred.

For the man of pre-capitalist societies, these presuppositions are alien ways, to be laboriously acquired. For the new system of dispositions is not constructed in a vacuum; it is built up from customary dispositions which outlast the disappearance or disintegration of their economic bases and which can only be adapted to the demands of the new objective situation by means of a creative transformation. The discrepancy between the agents' habitus and the structures of the economy, which is relatively narrow in nascent capitalism as in advanced capitalist society, is here as wide as it can be. Because they do not change in the same rhythm

5. *Ibid.* pp. 345–6.

as the economic structures, dispositions and ideologies corresponding to different economic structures, still present or already swept away, coexist in the same society and sometimes even in the same individuals. But the complexity of the phenomena is further increased by the fact that some remnants of the pre-capitalist mode of production persist despite everything, and with them, the associated dispositions. It follows from this that, both at the level of the economic structures and at the level of dispositions, representations, and values, the same duality is to be observed, as if these societies were not contemporary with themselves.

The decision to take as the primary object of our analysis the process by which dispositions and ideologies are adapted to imported and imposed economic structures, i.e. the reinvention of a new system of dispositions under the pressure of economic necessity, does not imply falling into the psychologistic subjectivism of considering that the dispositions of the economic subjects generate the structure of the objective economic or social relations. Nor does it imply the essentialist ethnocentrism that is often associated with subjectivism, which tends to make the desire to maximize utility or preference the principle governing all economic activity. Although it does not express a universal regularity of economic activity, the theory of marginal utility manifests a fundamental aspect of modern societies, the tendency towards (formal) "rationalization" which affects all facets of modern life. "The historical particularity of the capitalist epoch", wrote Weber, "and, by the same token, the significance of the theory of marginal utility (as of every economic value theory) for the understanding of this epoch, lies in the fact that, whereas the economic history of many past epochs has, not incorrectly, been termed 'the history of the uneconomic', in modern living conditions the approximation of reality to the theoretical propositions has been constantly increasing, involving the fate of ever broader strata of humanity, and, so far as one can foresee, will become steadily greater in the future. In this cultural-historical fact...lies the heuristic significance of the theory of marginal utility."[6]

The recent history of Algerian society is a particular case of this cultural-historical fact. The process of adaptation to the capitalist

6. Max Weber, "Die Grenznutlehre und das 'psychophysische Grundgesetz'" [1908], *Gesammelte Aufsätze zur Wissenschaftslehre*, 2nd edn (Tübingen: Mohr, 1951), p. 395.

economy which is to be observed there reminds us of what we are liable to forget if we consider only advanced capitalist societies, namely that the functioning of any economic system is tied to the existence of a definite system of dispositions towards the world, and, more precisely, towards time: because the economic system and the agents' dispositions are there in relative harmony, with "rationalization" extending little by little into the domestic economy, one is liable to forget that the economic system presents itself as a field of objective expectations which can only be fulfilled by agents endowed with a certain type of economic and, more broadly, temporal dispositions. Consequently, though description of the fully realized capitalist system can (at least as a first approximation) be restricted to objective properties, such as predictability and calculability, the fact remains that in developing societies, the discrepancy between the objective structures and the agents' dispositions is such that constructing an adequate economic theory would perhaps require one to refrain, in this case at least, from deducing behaviour from the system as it is or, worse, as one would like it to be.

Furthermore, when one observes the dramatic confrontation between an economic cosmos imposing itself and economic agents whom nothing has prepared to grasp its deep intention, one is forced to reflect on the conditions for the existence and functioning of the capitalist system, i.e. on the economic dispositions which it both favours and demands. Nothing, indeed, is more alien (or unimportant) to economic theory than the concrete economic subject: far from economics being a department of anthropology, anthropology is only an appendix to economics and *homo economicus* the result of an *a priori* style of deduction which tends to find confirmation in experience, at least statistically, because an economic system undergoing "rationalization" has the means to mould agents in accordance with its requirements. When one has implicitly or explicitly set oneself the problem of what economic man must be in order for the capitalist economy to be possible, one is inclined to consider the categories of the economic consciousness proper to the capitalist as universal categories, independent of economic and social conditions; and, by the same token, one runs the risk of ignoring the genesis, both collective and individual, of the structures of the economic consciousness.

Adaptation to an economic and social order, of whatever sort, presupposes an ensemble of knowledges transmitted by diffuse or formal education, practical skills and know-how bound up with an ethos and making it possible to act with a reasonable chance of success. Thus, adaptation to an economic organization which tends to ensure predictability and calculability demands a particular disposition towards time and, more precisely, towards the future, since the "rationalization" of economic conduct implies that the whole of existence be organized in relation to an absent, imaginary vanishing point. To understand the process of adapting to the capitalist economy, and in particular to explain its slowness and difficulty, it seems necessary to analyse, albeit briefly, the structure of the temporal consciousness associated with the pre-capitalist economy.

1 ❧ Simple reproduction and cyclical time

It is true that nothing is more foreign to the pre-capitalist economy than representation of the future (*le futur*) as a field of possibles to be explored and mastered by calculation. But it does not follow from this, as has often been supposed, that the Algerian peasant is incapable of fixing his sights on a distant future (*un avenir*), since his distrust of any attempt to take possession of the future always coexists with the foresight needed to spread the yield from a good harvest over a period of time, sometimes several years. The fact that the peasant sets aside for future consumption a proportion of his direct goods (that is to say, those goods capable of giving immediate satisfaction at any time, such as the consumption goods with which he surrounds himself and which constitute the tangible guarantee of his security) presupposes that he is aiming at a "forthcoming" future (*un "à venir"*) implicit in the directly perceived present. By contrast, the accumulation of indirect goods which, without being the source of any intrinsic satisfaction, can help to produce direct goods, is only meaningful in relation to a future (*un futur*) constructed by calculation. "Forecasting", said Cavaillès, "does not mean seeing things in advance" ("Prévoir, ce n'est pas voir à l'avance"). Fore-sight (*pré-voyance*) differs from forecasting in that the "forthcoming" (*l'avenir*) which it grasps is inherent in the situation itself as perceived through the technico-ritual schemes of perception and assessment inculcated by material conditions of existence, themselves grasped through the same schemes of thought. Economic decision is not determined here by taking into account a goal explicitly posited as future like that established by calculation within the framework of a plan; economic action is oriented towards a "forthcoming" that is directly grasped in experience or established by all the accumulated experiences which constitute the tradition.

Thus, in general, the peasant spends in relation to the income derived from the last harvest, and not the income expected from the next. Moreover, when the crop yields a surplus, he tends to treat the extra wheat or barley as direct goods and prefers to hoard them for consumption at a later date rather than sow them and increase his chances of getting a good yield from a future crop. He thus sacrifices future production to future consumption. Far from being dictated by a prospective aiming at a projected future, the practices of fore-sight stem from the desire to conform to inherited models. Thus the point of honour demands that, even if a peasant has no pomegranate trees, a stock of pomegranate seeds should be kept for use in the couscous served to his *khammes* or neighbours the first time the oxen go out for ploughing; likewise, it demands that salt meat should be kept in store for feastdays. Again, in the past, the mistress of the house would take pride in building up a special stock called *thiji*, made up of all the best produce, the best fruit (figs, raisins, pomegranates, nuts, etc.), the oil from the best olives, the best butter, and so on.[1] In this domain as elsewhere, ethical norms are also, and inseparably, ritual imperatives, and the homology between the fertilitiy of the house and the fertility of the land means that the hoarding of goods, which ensures the fullness of the house (*la'mmara ukham*), is as much a propitiatory rite as an economic act. Similarly, a number of practices which might seem to be investments obey a logic which is not that of economic calculation. Thus, land purchases, which became more frequent as the economic bases of the old society collapsed with the generalization of monetary exchange and the accompanying crisis of the peasant ethos, were, until recently, often motivated by the desire to prevent family land falling into the hands of another family. Similarly, the sense of honour has inspired many innovations in the field of agricultural and domestic equipment in the last fifty years, and it was not uncommon for the rivalry between the two factions into which most villages are divided, or between two great families, to lead both groups to provide themselves with the same equipment, oil presses, motor-driven mills, lorries, etc., without regard for profitability.

1. The dominance of the market economy brings about a complete reversal of the hierarchy of values expressed in this tradition. On the one hand, the top-quality products are needed for the market, and on the other hand, new patterns of consumption are adopted which help to justify abandoning the tradition of *thiji* and seeking cash incomes (for instance, the adoption of coffee, which has supplanted figs).

In an agrarian economy in which the production cycle can be encompassed in a single glance, since the products are generally renewed in the space of a year, the peasant no more dissociates his labour from the "forthcoming" product with which it is "pregnant" than, within the farming year, he distinguishes labour time from production time, a period when his activity is virtually suspended. By contrast, the capitalist economy, with its generally much longer production cycle, presupposes the constitution of a mediated, abstract future, with rational calculation having to make up for the absence of an intuitive grasp of the process as a whole. But for such calculation to be possible, the gap between labour time and production time has to be reduced, and with it the corresponding dependence on organic processes. In other words, the organic unity which united the present of labour with its "forthcoming" has to be broken. This unity is none other than that of the indivisible, unanalysable *cycles of reproduction*, or that of the product itself, as is seen by comparing a craft technique, making whole products, with industrial technology based on specialization and the parcelling-out of tasks. It is understandable that measures tending to change the traditional length of the agrarian cycles and requiring the sacrifice of an immediate tangible interest for the sake of an abstract interest (such as the offer to farmers to construct terraces, free of charge, for tree planting), were resisted by the Algerian peasants; they only began to show some (slight) interest when they saw the success of the improvements carried out on the lands of the European colonists, who had taken advantage of the offer without hesitation. More generally, if plans often arouse only incomprehension or scepticism, the reason is that, being based on abstract calculation and entailing a suspension of adherence to the familiar "given", they are tainted with the unreality of the imaginary. As if rational planning were to traditional fore-sight as rational demonstration in geometry is to a practical "showing" by cutting and folding, a project will only be accepted if it offers concrete, immediately perceptible results or if it is recommended by a recognized, respected "guarantor" (such as the schoolmaster in Kabyle villages).

Similarly, the deep distrust which the Algerian peasants long showed towards money is explained by the fact that, in terms of the temporal structures which it demands, monetary exchange is to barter as accumulation of capital is to hoarding.

Exchanges were formerly made in kind, in accordance with traditional rates of equivalence: "In the Tell region, the nomad would exchange one measure of dates for three measures of barley, or half a measure of wheat for three measures of dates."[2] In 1939, according to Augustin Berque, the rates were as follows: one quintal of wheat = one sheep = twenty litres of oil = two quintals of grapes or apricots = three hundred kilos of charcoal = one and a third quintals of barley. Until the Second World War, *khammes* and associates were paid in kind, and loans were made in kind, in most villages in Kabylia. The smith was paid for his work in cereals; pottery was until recently exchanged for the amount of figs or grain it could hold. In some places, exchange in kind has been kept up, but it has been reinterpreted in accordance with the logic of monetary exchange. Thus, wheat being worth twice as much in spring as at harvest time, the borrower must give back twice as much grain as he received. Only fifty years ago, market trading everywhere tended to be conducted through direct exchange of commodities rather than through commercial exchanges requiring the use of credit or cash. When money did play a part, it was mainly a standard for reference. Thus the quoted cash prices of products continued for a long time to reproduce their exchange rate as established at a time when transactions were conducted through barter.

Whereas the object exchanged offers directly to intuition the use that can be made of it, as an inherent quality along with its weight, colour, and taste, money, the indirect good *par excellence*, is in itself the source of no satisfaction (a fact underlined by the story of the fellah who died in the middle of the desert beside the sheepskin full of gold coins which he had just discovered). The future use to which it points is distant, imaginary, and undeterminate. And with paper money, one no longer possesses even the signs of things, but only the signs of signs. "A product", the saying runs, "is worth more than its equivalent [in money]." "Gather products rather than money." Money, which serves anyone, anywhere, for any exchange, an instrument "whose only use is to be useful for everything", enables its owner, on the one hand, to look forward to an indeterminate use and to quantify the infinity of possible uses it contains, so that a sort of accountancy of hopes can take place. "Though I don't know how much wheat I shall be able to buy with my money", Simiand observes, "I do know that I can buy some in the future; and if wheat isn't what I need, I know

2. A. Bernard and N. Lacroix, *L'évolution du nomadisme en Algérie* (Algiers: A. Jourdan, 1906), p. 207.

I shall be able to feed and clothe myself, and turn my gold to good purpose." And again: "This power to anticipate or represent a future value, even to realize it in advance, is the essential function of money, especially in progressive societies."[3] On the other hand, because the different uses to which a given sum can be put are mutually exclusive as soon as one sets about realizing them, the rational spending of a limited amount of money entails a calculation tending, first, to decide which future uses are possible within the limits of the means available, and which of these are mutually compatible, and secondly, to define the "reasonable" option in terms of a hierarchy of goals. By contrast, commodities exchanged in barter on the basis of traditional equivalences immediately declare their potential use and their value, which, unlike that of money, is independent of all external conditions. It is therefore much easier to manage reserves of consumption goods "reasonably" than to spread a sum of money over a whole month or draw up a rational hierarchy of needs and expenditure. Clearly, the tendency to consume everything is infinitely less great than the temptation to realize all one's money at once. The Kabyles keep their wheat and barley in large earthenware jars made with holes at various heights, and the prudent mistress of the house, responsible for managing the reserves, knows that when the level of the grain falls below the central hole, called *thimith*, the navel, she must curb consumption. The "calculation" is automatic and the jar functions like an hour-glass showing at all times how much has gone and how much is left. In short, the use of money demands a conversion comparable to that effected in another context by analytical geometry: the apodictic evidence of the senses is ousted by the "blind self-evidence" derived from the manipulation of symbols. Henceforward, instead of handling objects which declare almost tangibly and palpably the use and satisfaction which they promise, reason deals with signs which in themselves are the source of no pleasure. Between the economic subject and the commodities or services he seeks falls the veil of money. Economic agents brought up to an older economic logic therefore have to learn, at their own expense, the rational use of money as the universal mediation of economic relations. They are sorely tempted to

3. F. Simiand, "La monnaie, réalité sociale", *Annales Sociologiques*, ser. D, 1934, pp. 81 and 80.

convert all their wages, as soon as they get them, into real goods, food, clothing, furniture, and so on, and fifty years ago it was not uncommon to see farm workers spending a month's pay in a few days. More recently, similar behaviour was observed among the southern nomads, when the shepherds, who had previously been paid in kind, started to be paid a wage in cash.

It is also certain that the peasants' lack of skill in handling money and inability to adjust to legal rules have played an important part in accelerating the process by which they have been dispossessed of their land. Thus, after condemning the policy which was divesting the Algerians of their common land, Violette observed: "Far too much use is made of expropriation... When there are grounds for expropriating, at least there should be fair compensation, and the authorities should carry out their duty to resettle those expropriated, especially the natives ...Cash compensation is meaningless to the fellah. He will spend it immediately; he is not capable of investing it and using the modest income he would get from the interest."[4] A number of small landowners, who had acquired documents giving readily negotiable property rights as a result of the breakup of formerly undivided estates that was encouraged by the laws of 1873 and 1897, were tempted by their poverty to sell their lands. Unused to handling money, they soon squandered their modest capital and were forced to work for wages as farm hands or to migrate to the towns.

Of all the economic institutions and techniques introduced by colonization, the one most alien to the logic of the pre-capitalist economy is undoubtedly *credit*, which entails reference to an abstract future defined by a written contract that is guaranteed by a whole system of sanctions, and which, with the notion of interest, brings in the financial value of time.

Usury, with average interest rates of 50 to 60 per cent before 1830 and 25 to 30 per cent in 1867,[5] certainly had a part to play in an economy which, though minimizing the role of money circulation, was constantly subject to crises owing to the vagaries of the climate, which the available techniques could do little to mitigate. But this emergency credit, imposed by necessity and used exclusively for consumption, was quite different from credit used for investment. The usurer is the last resort, after all the resources of family mutual aid have been exhausted, and anyone who forced a brother or cousin to go to the usurer when he could have given aid himself would have been dishonoured. The prohibition of interest on loans is simply the counterpart of the imperative of solidarity, and the community rules, sometimes codified as customary laws, required assistance to be given to the sick, widows, orphans, and the poor, and also to the victims of misfortune (for example, when an injured animal had to be slaughtered, the

4. M. Violette, *L'Algérie vivra-t-elle? Notes d'un ancien gouverneur général* (Paris: Alcan, 1931), pp. 83–91.
5. A. Hanoteau, *Poésies populaires de la Kabylie* (Paris: Imprimerie Impériale, 1867), p. 193 n. 1.

community compensated the owner and the meat was shared among the families).

Whereas credit takes care to guarantee its security by making sure of the debtor's solvency, amicable agreements (the only ones recognized by the ethic of honour) are backed solely by good faith, the assurances for the future being provided not by wealth but by the owner of the wealth. The prospective borrower calls on a relative or friend and says, "I know you have such a sum and that you don't need it. You can look upon it as still being in your house." No precise date is fixed for repayment ("in the summer" or "after the harvest"). Since such arrangements are only made between acquaintances, whether kinsmen, friends, or affines, the future of the association is ensured, in the present itself, not only by each party's experience of the other, whom he knows to be reliable, but also by the objective relationship between the partners, which will outlast their transaction, guaranteeing the future of the exchange more surely than any of the explicit, formal codifications with which credit must arm itself because it presupposes the complete impersonality of the relationship between contracting parties. Nothing is more antithetical to mutual aid, which always associates individuals united by ties of real or fictitious kinship, than the co-operation which mobilizes individuals selected with a view to the calculated aims of a specific undertaking. In mutual aid, the group exists before and after the shared performance of a shared task; in co-operation, the group's *raison d'être* lies outside itself, in the future goal defined by the contract, and it ceases to exist as soon as the contract is fulfilled. In other words, contrary to populist illusions, the traditions of agnate mutual aid are far from preparing the peasants to adapt to co-operative or collectivist forms of organization; the agricultural workers in intensively colonized areas, who have been dispossessed of their land and their traditions, are more amenable to this type of structure than the smallholders of relatively uncolonized regions.

What distinguishes the indefinite future (*le futur*), the locus of the abstract possibles of an interchangeable subject, from the practical, "forthcoming" future (*l'avenir pratique*), the possible of *objective potentiality*, is not, as is often supposed, a greater or lesser distance from the present, since the latter can put forward as quasi-present the potentialities, variously remote in objective time,

The disenchantment of the world

that are linked to it in the immediate unity of a practice or a natural cycle. The popular consciousness experiences and enacts this distinction without explicitly stating it, except in the form of self-irony. "Where are you going?" his friends asked Djeha, an imaginary character with whom the Kabyles like to identify. "I'm going to market." "What! Shouldn't you add, 'If it please God'?" Djeha went on his way, but when he came to a wood, he was beaten and robbed by brigands. "Where are you going, Djeha?" "I'm going home", said Djeha, "...if it please God." The phrase indicates that one is moving into a different world, governed by a different logic, the unreal world of the future and its possibles.[6]

Perhaps we should see here one of the roots of the taboo on all forms of numerical assessment: the number of men present in an assembly must not be counted, the seedcorn must not be measured, the number of eggs laid must not be counted, but the chicks that have hatched are counted. To count the eggs laid or measure the seedcorn would be to presume upon the future and thereby to jeopardize it, to "cut" or "close" it. The fellah measures his harvest only with extreme precaution, "so as not to count God's generosity". In some regions it is forbidden to utter the name of a number on the threshing floor. Elsewhere, euphemistic numbers are used. Similarly, administrative attempts to carry out a census met with intense resistance at first. In a poem by Qaddoûr ben Klîfa quoted by Desparmet,[7] one finds this: "All our goods have been weighed in the balance. How many acres have been surveyed, measured with a yardstick! Every year we are set down on the census roll! They have recorded every living man and woman!" The same refusal of exact figures and calculation inspired nicknames applied to the French in poetry: "the industrious race", "the race of philosophers" (scientists), "the people of the signature and the rubber stamp".[8]

6. The story is told of an aged Kabyle who for the first time in his life reached the summit of a hill which marked the horizon of his village, and exclaimed: "O God, how great your world is." Beyond the horizon of the present begins the imaginary world which cannot be connected with the universe of experience and which is therefore governed by a quite different logic. Things that might appear absurd or impossible if they were located in the field of experience can come about in other places remote in space and time. This is true of the miracles of the saints; Sidi Yahia, who made a slaughtered ox stand up, Sidi Kali, who turned himself into a lion, Sidi Mouhoub, who divided a fountain to settle a dispute between two hostile clans, or Sidi Moussa, who caused olive oil to gush from a pillar. Different criteria apply to events occurring within the familiar horizon and to those in the land of legends which begins at the boundaries of the everyday world. In the first case, the only guarantee is the evidence of one's senses, or short of this, the authority of someone known and trustworthy. The second case involves a universe in which, by definition, anything is possible; here the criteria are much less strict, and any affirmation conveyed by the general opinion will be entertained.
7. J. Desparmet, "Les réactions nationalitaires en Algérie", *Bulletin de la Société de Géographie d'Alger*, 1933; see also "La turcophilie en Algérie", *ibid.* 1916.
8. Desparmet, "L'œuvre de la France jugée par les indigènes", *ibid.* 1910.

Aska d azqa, "tomorrow is the tomb": the future is a void which it would be futile to try to grasp, a nothingness which does not belong to us. The man who worries too much about the future, forgetting that it is beyond his reach, is said "to want to make himself the associate of God"; and to urge him to more restraint, people say, "Don't trouble yourself about what is foreign to you", or again: "When money's not in your purse, don't see it as capital."

The story of Djeha is sufficient to warn us against the ethnocentrism which leads so many anthropologists to establish an essential difference between the system of dispositions towards time which the pre-capitalist economy calls forth and the system required and created by the money-based economy. The temporal experience that is favoured by the pre-capitalist economy is one of the modalities which all experience of temporality can assume, including that of the most "rational" economic agents in the societies which produce anthropologists. It owes its specificity solely to the fact that instead of presenting itself as one possibility among others, it is imposed as the *only possible* experience by an economy which is unable to provide the conditions in which it is possible to posit the notion of the possible and, which amounts to the same thing, by an ethos which is nothing other than the internalization of the system of possibilities and impossibilities objectively inscribed in material conditions of existence dominated by insecurity and accident. Everything takes place as if explicit discouragement of all the dispositions demanded and favoured by the capitalist economy – the spirit of enterprise, concern for productivity and efficiency, etc. – and denunciation of the spirit of forecasting as devilish ambition, on the grounds that "the future is in God's hands", were simply ways of "making a virtue of necessity", here as elsewhere, and of adjusting one's hopes to the objective probabilities.

If the economic practices of the Algerian peasant can only be understood in terms of the categories of his temporal consciousness, the fact remains that those categories are closely linked, through the mediation of the ethos, to the economic bases of the society. The aim of technical and ritual activity is to ensure what

Marx termed simple reproduction, in other words the production of the goods which enable the group to subsist and to reproduce itself biologically, and, inseparably from this, the reproduction of the ties, values, and beliefs which ensure the cohesion of the group.

Economy and ethos are so profoundly interdependent that the whole attitude towards time, calculation, and forecasting is virtually inscribed in the mode of appropriating the soil, namely joint ownership and joint exploitation. It has often been pointed out that in preventing calculation of the respective share of each member of the group (or each household) in consumption and, *a fortiori*, in production, this institution tends to prevent individual invention and stifle enterprise.[9] In the area of consumption, it allows calculation to be reduced to its simplest expression, i.e. a fairly flexible rationing, without there ever being any measurement of the relation between resources and the number of individuals. Among other consequences, it follows that there is no brake on the birth rate.[10] But, equally, undivided ownership can only continue so long as no one thinks of drawing up a systematic balance-sheet of the individual shares in production and consumption. And indeed the generalization of money exchanges and of the spirit of calculation has everywhere coincided with an increasing number of breakups of joint ownership; by making it possible to measure and compare the energy expended, the product of labour and the resources consumed, money encourages calculation of the respective share of each household in the group economy. In short, joint ownership in fact prevents calculation, and, conversely, the prevention of calculation is the condition of the permanence of undivided property and of the community (family or clan) that is based on it.

It is remarkable to see how the ethos is carried straight through

9. I realize the ethnocentric character of such a view. For an analysis of the various functions of undivided ownership in the economic system of pre-colonial Algeria, see P. Bourdieu, *Sociologie de l'Algérie* (Paris: PUF, 1960), p. 66.
10. There is a need for a systematic study of the differential influence which the various inheritance systems and modes of land appropriation which accompany them (primogeniture, ownership reserved for a single heir, equal shares, whether parcelled out or, as in Algeria, held jointly) have exerted or now exert on the birth rate, the spirit of enterprise, emigration to towns, etc. (cf. H. J. Habakkuk, "Family Structure and Economic Change in Nineteenth-Century Europe", *Journal of Economic History*, 15 (1955), 1–12.

into ethics. The precepts of the mode of honour which denounce the spirit of calculation and all its manifestations, such as avidity and haste, which condemn the tyranny of the watch, "the devil's mill", can be seen as so many partial and veiled formulations of the objective "intention" of the economy. Since exchanges are reduced to the minimum, they cannot become the focal point around which production and consumption might be organized; each production unit tends to live self-sufficiently, so that most exchanges take place between close acquaintances and it would be absurd to bring calculation into them; the producer, being at the same time the consumer, does not assess his production in terms of the effort or time spent on it. Wastage of time – which appears as such only by reference to alien principles, such as the principle of maximum profitability – and wastage of means are perhaps the condition of the survival of societies which, if they counted, would give up.

Certainly calculation is necessarily implied in every equitable transaction. Let us consider a type of association that is common practice in dealing with livestock. The owner (often a woman who has invested her savings in this way) entrusts her animals, goats for example, to another person, who promises to feed and look after them. The animals are evaluated and it is agreed that the produce from them will be shared. Every week the borrower sends a gourd of milk which is delivered by a child (who receives in return fruit, oil, eggs, or sugar). After three years, the borrower returns the animals and the profits are shared between the two parties, as is the diminution of the original capital due to ageing: either the borrower pays compensation in kind, or he gives back only half the flock together with a sum equal to half its value at the beginning of the contract. It can be seen that although such an arrangement is only possible between acquaintances, among friends, and although it is always an occasion for ritual exchanges totally foreign to the spirit of calculation, it never steps outside the most strict calculation.

But calculation is in the service of the sense of equity and is absolutely opposed to the *spirit of calculation* which, relying on the quantitative evaluation of profit, abolishes the hazardous and (at least apparently) disinterested approximations of a code of generosity and honour. It is acceptable only if subordinated to the sense of equity which has its roots in the punctilious egalitarianism of the point of honour rather than in a rational, abstract consciousness of equality. Similarly, if innovation is always suspect – and not only inasmuch as it flouts tradition – this is because the peasants are always inclined to see it as the desire to distinguish oneself, to stand apart, a way of challenging others and crushing them. The demand for conformity can thus be understood within the logic of honour: to stand apart from others, especially by gratuitous and ostentatious novelty, is to throw down a challenge to the group and its point of honour; like the gift so great as to rule out a counter-gift, ostentatious conduct (or conduct perceived as such) puts the group into a state of inferiority and can only be felt as an affront, each member feeling an attack on his self-esteem.

The acquisition of wealth is never explicitly recognized as the goal of economic activity. Resistance to accumulation and to the accompanying differentiation is a way of safeguarding the economic bases of the social order, since, in a stationary economy in which the quantity of assets possessed (i.e. mainly land) is constant, one man's enrichment is another man's impoverishment. And, once again, the ethic simply records the necessities immanent in the economy.

"A generous man", the Kabyles say, "is God's friend." God gives wealth to whom he chooses, but he who receives must show himself worthy of it by proving his generosity, by using his wealth to alleviate the poverty of others; otherwise he will be denied wealth. "My God, give unto me", another saying runs, "that I may give." "My God, if thou givest not to me, give to my brother." The man who can combine wealth, generosity and sobriety (*aqnâ*) is the happiest of men, for the world and the hereafter belong to him. Wealth entails duties. Wealth unaccompanied by generosity is despised.

Though never absent, calculation is never avowed. Certain tasks, such as harvesting, olive gathering, hoeing, and second dressing, were performed in Kabylia by the sub-clan, the clan, and sometimes the whole village; the same was true of the transporting of stones and beams when a new house was being built. After the opening rites, the placing of objects in the foundations, and the sacrifices which marked the start and the completion of the work and which were performed by the head of the family, after the annointing of the materials with the blood of the victim, the work ended with a shared meal in which the sacrificed animal was eaten.

When the meal was over the women sang in alternating choirs while the girls danced. Shared work was a collective rite and feast through which family solidarity was publicly and solemnly reaffirmed. But the economic consequences of the feast were weighty; a single meal might swallow up the laboriously amassed provisions. In principle, all the inhabitants of the village who had helped with the building ought to take part. In reality, depending on the locality, only the notables were invited, or one man per family, or the members of the same clan or same sub-clan.[11] Thus, calculation was used to solve the problem posed by calculation; but people could not but approve a use of calculation which tended to perpetuate traditions incompatible with the spirit of calculation.

The generalization of monetary exchanges has had the better of a number of these traditions. When houses were built, the masonry and carpentry were entrusted to specialists who were compensated in kind or in cash: the meal was never taken into account in estimating the wage; the workman might forgo the wage, but never the meal. In a village in the Sidi-Aïch region, a renowned mason who had learnt his trade in France was called to help build a house, in about 1955; he went home without having the meal and requested 200 francs indemnity. He was immediately paid for the day's labour (1,000 francs), together with the 200 francs, and was told never to return.[12] The story spread and since then people have been reluctant to give him any work at all. This anecdote contains the essence of the debate between – inevitable – calculation and the – blameworthy – spirit of calculation. It shows that a clear-cut distinction is drawn between payment in kind or in cash, as compensation for the effort supplied (which may come to be seen as a wage), and the meal, a symbolic act which cannot be reduced to its strictly economic dimension without causing a scandal. The meal is an act of exchange which seals an alliance, which unites strangers in a relationship analogous to kinship ("Between us I put the food and the salt"). *Thiwizi* (collective work) is inconceivable without the final meal. Therefore it only brings together people from the same clan or the same sub-clan. It is understandable that the mason provoked unanimous

11. R. Maunier, *Mélanges de sociologie nord-africaine* (Paris: Alcan, 1930), pp. 171–2.
12. Here, and subsequently in this text, the sums quoted are in old francs.

The disenchantment of the world

reproval: his conduct merely enacted in complete logic the calculative intention that was expressed in a disguised form through the artifices used to limit the expense; but, by drawing all the inferences, demanding the conversion of the meal into money, it brought out into broad daylight that which the approved conduct contrived to conceal. For the rule of the game is that objective convertibility and calculability must never appear as such.

There are exchanges in which calculation betrays itself rather more, for example *charka*, a contract generally agreed between men of different villages, whereby the owner of an ox entrusts it to a peasant too poor to buy one, in exchange for a certain number of measures of wheat or barley. It might seem that in this case the ox is treated like capital (*ras elmal*, literally, "the head of the chattel") intended to yield a profit. But in fact the discrepancy between the objective truth of the economic exchange and the experience the agents have of it is never more manifest. The economist can see this exchange as a simple loan, individual A entrusting an ox to individual B in return for a quantity of wheat by way of interest. The description the Kabyles give of it is very different: individual A gives the ox's labour-power, but equity is satisfied because individual B feeds the ox, which individual A would have had to do in any case. The measures of wheat are then nothing other than a compensation for the ox's loss of value due to ageing. It can thus be seen that the ox is never perceived and treated as capital (it is not uncommon for a borrower who wants to conceal his poverty and to have it thought that the ox is his own to deliver the wheat prescribed in the contract by night; and for the owner to play along with him because it is best to be discreet about a transaction which bears within it the potentiality of exploitation). When self-interested calculation is openly revealed, it is sharply reproved: this happens in the case of a certain type of *rahnia* (mortgage), a contract whereby the borrower grants the lender the usufruct of a piece of land until the date of repayment. However, things are not always so clear-cut, and there is room for a whole casuistry. No one would condemn – far from it – a man who lends money to a kinsman in difficulty in return for land treated as security. (The sum lent may bear no relation to the value of the land; it may be greater or smaller, depending on the borrower's needs. So there is no calculation; nor is any deadline fixed for taking possession of the land.) "You've saved me from having to sell" is what is said in such cases. Preventing land from falling into the hands of strangers is a duty; and since the land is never really treated as capital, it is implicitly accepted that the produce from it should go to the man who works on it.

Thus, at the risk of always remaining in ambiguity and equivocation, people play simultaneously in the registers of unavowed self-interest and publicly declared honour. Is the generous exchange anything other than the unfolding in temporal succession of the different moments of a transaction which the rational contract telescopes into an instant? If the gift can appear to the observer as an obligatory stage in a continuous series of gifts and counter-gifts, whereas it is experienced as a disinterested, deliberate act, this is precisely by virtue of the time-lag interposed. The worst offence is precisely that of immediately returning the gift received or giving back an identical object. Because the counter-gift is deferred, each act of giving can be grasped as an absolute beginning and not as the forced continuation of an exchange already begun. Everything takes place as if generous exchange tended to allow the actors in the transaction not to have to discover it *as* a transaction – not to have to recognize inwardly or before others the existence of the *model* in accordance with which they objectively act. Gift exchange is an exchange in and by which the agents strive to conceal the objective truth of the exchange, i.e. the calculation which guarantees the equity of the exchange. If "fair exchange", the direct swapping of equivalent values, is the truth of gift exchange, gift exchange is a swapping which cannot acknowledge itself as such.[13] It is therefore the

13. This analysis points the way beyond the opposition that Lévi-Strauss, for example, establishes between a "wordy phenomenology" held captive by the ideologies springing from the lived experience of exchange, and structural anthropology, which is able to reconstruct the model in accordance with which that experience occurs, at the cost of an objectivist break with the content of naive experience. "It is exchange that constitutes the basic phenomenon and not the discrete operations into which social life breaks it down" (C. Lévi-Strauss, "Introduction à l'œuvre de Mauss", in M. Mauss, *Sociologie et anthropologie* (Paris: PUF, 1950), pp. xxxviii, xxxix, xlvi). The anthropologist has the task of reconstituting the totality from which it is possible to discover the unity between subjective experience, a distorted apprehension of the social system, and the objective structure which scientific reflection constructs or discovers. Indeed, only the existence of an essential discrepancy between subjective certainty and objective truth can explain how the gift can be described as a moment in an indefinite series of prestations and counter-prestations and, at the same time, be experienced as a deliberate, disinterested act.

exchange form *par excellence* in a society which, in Lukács's phrase, denies "the true soil of its life" and which, unwilling to confer on economic realities their specifically and purely economic meaning, has an *economy in itself* and not for itself. In systematically accentuating the symbolic significance of the acts or relations of production, this society refuses to posit the economy as such, i.e. as a system governed by laws of its own, and to recognize explicitly the economic goals by reference to which economic action is objectively oriented, those of self-interested calculation, competition, or exploitation.

The same *negation* is observed in production. The peasant does not arise as an effective power confronting an alien world: very close to a nature that is neither prepared for nor marked by the action of man, he can only feel submissiveness before forces he does not aspire to discipline. Is it surprising that he does not understand his own action as *labour* in the true sense of the word, that he refuses to treat as a raw material the omnipotent nature which his beliefs people with charms and mysteries, which is the dwelling of a diffuse, impersonal sacredness, the source of all misfortunes and all benefits? The peasant does not, strictly speaking, labour: he takes pains. "Give [your sweat] to the earth, and she will give to you", says the proverb. This can be taken to mean that nature, obedient to the logic of gift exchange, grants her benefits only to those who bring her their toil in tribute. But more profoundly, it could be that technical action is a form of revivification ritual.[14] It is in fact the application of categories foreign to the peasant's experience that produces the distinction between the technical aspect and the ritual aspect of farming activity. Performed within a cosmic cycle which they punctuate, the tasks of farming, such as ploughing or harvesting, impose themselves with the arbitrary rigour of traditional duties, with the same necessity as the rites which are inseparable from them. Never treated as a common substance or raw material to be exploited, the earth is the object of a respect mingled with fear (*el hiba*). It

---

14. The old folk describe the abandonment of farming traditions as a scandal, a profanation, and a sacrilege. For example, to leave it to youngsters, as happens more and more often, to "open the earth and plough into it the wealth of the new year", is an insult to the land. "The earth no longer gives anything because it is given nothing. People openly mock the land and it is only right that the land should pay us back with lies."

is said that the land will "settle its scores" and get its own back for the ill-treatment it receives at the hands of the over-hasty or clumsy peasant (*el ah'maq*). The truth of agrarian practices and of the ethos which inhabits them finds symbolic expression in the ritual system, whose buried intention can be brought out by structural analysis. Left to itself, nature tends leftwards, towards fallowness and sterility. Like twisted, malignant woman, it must be subjected to the beneficent, fertilizing action of man. Although necessary and inevitable, this intervention by the peasant and his techniques is criminal, because it is rape and violence. Everything takes place as if the rites, particularly those which mark the critical points in the relation between man and the earth, ploughing and harvesting, were informed by the intention of resolving the contradiction at the heart of farming, which is forced to violate the earth in order to tear its riches from it.[15]

Work is neither an end in itself nor a virtue *per se*. What is valued is not action directed towards an economic goal, but activity in itself, regardless of its economic function and merely on condition that it has a social function. The self-respecting man must always be busy doing something. If he can find nothing to do, "at least he can carve his spoon". "The unoccupied shepherd", runs another saying, "carves his stick". A lazy person is not fulfilling the function incumbent upon him as a member of the group: he thereby sets himself on the edge of society and runs the risk of being cast out. To remain idle, especially if one belongs to a great family, is to fall down on one's commitments to the group, to avoid the duties, tasks, and responsibilities that are inseparable from membership in the group. So, for example, a man who has been out of farming activity for some time, whether on account of illness or emigration to France, is rapidly reinstated on his return into the cycle of work and the circuit of the exchange of services. The adolescents of poor families, the sons of widows, are told: "Go and hire yourselves out (*charkath*), you'll become men by holding the plough and digging the earth." Because the group is entitled to demand of everyone that he undertake an occupation, it is also obliged to make sure that everyone *has* an occupation,

15. On this point, see P. Bourdieu, "Generative Schemes and Practical Logic: Invention within Limits", *Outline of a Theory of Practice* (Cambridge: University Press, 1977), chap. 3, pp. 96–158.

albeit a purely symbolic one. The farmer who provides an opportunity to work on his land for those who have no land to plough, no plough to hold, no trees to prune, such as the sons of *khammes*, farm labourers, or widows, is universally approved, because he is giving these marginal individuals a chance to integrate themselves into the group, in short, to become complete men.

In such a context, what must appear as a state of merely being occupied when one implicitly relates it to the conception of labour as productive activity, was not and could not be perceived in that way. Thus, the head of the family was naturally the oldest member, because his work, in his own eyes and in those of the group, was identified with the very function of head of the family, responsible for each and for all, charged with ordering and organizing work, expenditure, and social relations. The distinction between productive and unproductive labour, like the distinction between profitable and unprofitable labour, was relegated to the background; the fundamental opposition was between the idler (by circumstance or inclination) who fails in his social duty and the worker who fulfils his social function, whatever the product of his efforts. The true peasant would be recognized by the fact that he devoted every moment of respite to the little tasks which were, so to speak, the art for art's sake of the peasant art of living – fencing the fields, pruning the trees, protecting the young shoots against animals, or "visiting" and watching over the fields; in the absence of concern for profitability and productivity, effort was both its own yardstick and its own end.

If a clear-cut distinction is not made between work as gainful activity and work as a social function, one is likely to fail to understand the logic of pre-capitalist economies. Max Weber himself invited misunderstanding by his use of the equivocal concept *Beruf*. In fact, depending on the point of view adopted, it is possible to consider that bourgeois capitalism, like the Protestant ethic, makes work an end in itself, activity being not a mere economic means, *qua* gainful activity, but a moral end, *qua* ethically imposed duty; or, conversely, that the ultimate end of existence is not, for the capitalist, work as an end in itself, but "work as a means of earning more and more money", the fundamental imperative being "the individual's duty to increase his capital". This second aspect is the one Weber himself emphasizes in the texts he devotes to the traditionalist spirit: "The universal reign of absolute unscrupulousness in the pursuit of selfish interests by the making of money has been a specific characteristic of precisely those countries whose bourgeois-capitalistic development, measured according to Occidental standards, has remained backward. As every employer knows, the lack of *coscienziosità* of the labourers of such countries, for instance Italy as compared with Germany, has been, and to a certain extent still is, one of the principal obstacles to their capitalistic development."[16] What is in question here is an ethic of work considered as gainful activity. Elsewhere, Weber rightly remarks that what distinguishes "traditionalist" societies is that there the appetite for gain does not constitute *per se* an incitement to work. But it must not be forgotten that work *qua* social function is one of the traditional duties.

However inefficient it may be, the peasant's action transforms nature by doing it violence; but it cannot appear to him in that light. Such a self-avowal presupposes a conversion of the relation between man and the world: convinced that he has no means of acting effectively on his future and on the future of his production, the peasant feels himself responsible only for the act, not for its success or failure, which depend on natural or supernatural powers. Labour as such appears when (and only when) the self-remission that is indissociable from dependence gives way to avowed aggression against a nature stripped of the enchantments of magic and reduced to its economic dimension alone. Farming activity then ceases to be a tribute paid to a necessary order; it is labour, i.e. action directed towards another possible order which can only come through the transformation of the present given order. So long as the distinction between the social function of the effort and its strictly economic function remains unknown, activity cannot explicitly direct itself towards an exclusively economic goal. But deliberate, systematic organization of all economic means in relation to a common goal, monetary profit, is the precondition for the emergence of an economic order dominated by the necessity of obtaining a cash profit, a strictly economic necessity independent of ethical imperatives.

The disenchantment of the world coincides with the failure of the endeavour to enchant the experience of time (*la durée*) by magico-ritual stereotyping of the techniques or rituals which tended to make the unfolding of time "the moving image of eternity". So long as activity has no other goal than to ensure reproduction of the economic and social order, so long as the whole group sets itself no other goal than to last, and objectively transforms the world without acknowledging that it does so, the

16. *The Protestant Ethic and the Spirit of Capitalism* (London: Unwin, 1930), p. 57.

acting subject lives in the very rhythm (*dure de la durée*) of the world with which he is bound up. He cannot discover himself as an historical agent whose action in the present, against the present order, is only meaningful in relation to the future and to the future order which it works to bring about. Traditionalism appears as a methodical undertaking (though not apparent to itself as such) aimed at denying the event *as* an event, i.e. as a novelty induced by innovatory action or tending to induce it; aimed at overcoming events by making chronological order depend on the eternal order of mythic logic.

The Kabyle peasant's existence is rhythmically structured by the divisions of the mythico-ritual calendar which is nothing other than the projection, into the order of succession, of the system of mythic oppositions which dominate the whole of existence. Autumn and winter are opposed to spring and summer as the wet is opposed to the dry, down to up, cold to hot, left to right, west and north to east and south, night to day, male to female. Ploughing and sowing are opposed to reaping and treading-out as weaving, the homologue of ploughing, is opposed to the firing of pottery, and so on. The organizing principle of the temporal succession is the same as that which determines the division of labour between the sexes, the distinction between the moist food of the wet season and the dry food of the dry season, the alternations of social life, feasts, rites, games, tasks, the organization of space, and numerous other features. Thus, two successive moments can be referred to the two opposing terms of a timeless relation; hence social time as form, in the musical sense, i.e. as the ordering of a succession, an order whose essence is that it is only accomplished within time, is reducible to a timeless system of logical oppositions.[17]

The calendar of tasks and feasts, which is both an organizing principle – with the function of ordering the temporal succession – and an integrating force, since it guarantees the harmonization of individual conducts and the mutual fulfilment of expectations about the behaviour of others, founds the cohesion of the group by forbidding any frustration of collective expectations at the same time as it ensures predictability, by means opposed to those of science or economic calculation. The social order is first of all a

---

17. On this point too, see Bourdieu. "Generative Schemes", *loc. cit.*

rhythm, a tempo. Conforming to the social order is primarily a matter of respecting rhythms, keeping pace, not getting out of step. Belonging to the group means behaving in the same way at the same time of the day and the year as the other members of the group. To adopt unusual rhythms and take eccentric paths is in itself to stand outside the group. Working when others are resting, staying at home when others are in the fields, strolling in the village streets when others are sleeping, walking along deserted roads, lingering in the streets when others are at the market – these are all suspicious ways of behaving. Respect for the temporal rhythms is indeed one of the fundamental imperatives of this ethic of conformity. Observance of the annual rhythms is even more rigorously required. Not only are the major dates of the farming year determined by collective decision and preceded by feasts and ceremonies, but every technical or social activity has its prescribed day and hour. The farming calendar sets out recommendations, taboos, proverbs, and portents for every period. The eccentric individual who behaves differently from others is called *amkhalef* (from *khalef*, to infringe, contravene); and it is pointed out, with a pun on the roots, that *amkhalef* is also the man who is late (from *khellef*, to leave behind). But untimely conduct not only infringes the imperative which condemns singularity; it transgresses the imperative which imposes conformity with a social order that is identical with the order of the world.

Like scientific reason, the pre-capitalist ethos endeavours to make sure of the future, but in very different ways. Forecasting entails recognizing the possibility of the unforeseen, the possibility of another possible which could contradict it: the hypothesis creates the event *as* an event, i.e. as a denial or confirmation. But the prudence of traditionalism will not be belied by the world. It does not form the ambition of taking hold of the future, it only strives to offer the future the least possible hold upon itself. The fear of an objective refutation, which could shake the established order and break the interlocking of expectations, leads people to hold fast to a state of affairs that can be mastered by the simple actualization of the traditional schemes, at the cost of a systematic contraction of the field of aspirations; and methodically to exclude the unusual situations which would demand the invention of new schemes. Adherence to an undisputed tradition implies refusal to engage openly in the struggle against nature and leads to the pursuit of equilibrium at the cost of a reduction of expectations commensurate with the weakness of the means of acting on the world. Constantly threatened in its very existence, forced to spend all its energy in maintaining a precarious equilibrium with the external world, this society, haunted by the concern with subsisting, chooses to conserve so as to conserve itself rather than transform itself so as to transform.

The traditional order is viable only on condition that it is apprehended, not as the best possible one, but as the only possible one – on condition that everyone remains unaware of the "lateral possibles" which contain the worst of threats in the very fact that they would show up the traditional order, held to be immutable and necessary, as one possible order among others, in other words, as arbitrary. The survival of traditionalism hangs on its not being aware of itself as such, that is, as a choice made unawares. In refusing projects and, by the same token, labour, in the sense of will directed towards transforming the world and the means of transforming the world, such a society refuses to have a history. For labour, like the pursuit of progress or the revolutionary consciousness, is based on the choice of adopting the perspective of the possible, of suspending passive acquiescence in the natural or social order. The will to transform the world entails transcending the present in the direction of a rationally calculated future which can only be attained by transforming present "given" reality and above all by transforming the transformative action, that is, techniques and the agents who use them. Traditionalism seeks to abolish chronological succession in the sense of continuous discontinuity, by reducing the chronological order (in the cycle of life as in the cycle of farming) to the (mytho)logical order. And perhaps structural analysis *unwittingly* reproduces the profoundest intention of this social order when it gathers together in the instant, in the form of a system of oppositions and homologies, what is by nature a succession; in this respect structural analysis can be said to resemble a Leibnizian God, capable of really comprehending the essence of the square root of 2, which the agents only ever grasp partially and successively by endlessly adding further figures after the decimal point.

2 ✣ Contradictory necessities and ambiguous conduct

Although the immense and extremely varied literature which anthropologists have devoted to culture change cannot be characterized generically without some degree of arbitrariness, it cannot fail to be observed that these studies, which differ profoundly in the objects they treat, generally concur in autonomizing certain levels of social reality and give only very limited space to economic transformations, in particular to systematic examination of the influence such transformations have on the system of social relations and dispositions. Whether the authors emphasize "cultural transactions", the logic of selectivity, the recontextualization of borrowings and the reinterpretation of original features, the phenomena of cultural disintegration or reintegration, the dynamics of the personality changes which result from changes in the techniques of early education, or the differential adaptability of the different cultures brought into contact, or whether they concern themselves rather with the relations between the societies involved, the type of social relations between the individuals who compose them, the concrete form of these relations (superiority or inferiority, distance or proximity, etc.), and the situation in which they are set up (a colonial situation, a reservation, etc.), they restrict themselves to culture change or social change in its generic form, generally failing to analyse the progressive differentiation of the society and the differential reactions of the different social classes.

But this "ethnological bias", which stems in part from the economic and social characteristics of the societies studied by "acculturation" specialists, is no doubt less dangerous than the systematic distortions which a certain type of sociology introduces by dissociating differences in attitudes to "modernism" and "modernization" from the economic and social conditions of their formation and expression. Thus, on the basis of a vast survey in six Middle Eastern countries, Daniel Lerner presents "a theory of modernization that articulates the common compulsions to which all Middle Eastern peoples are subject",[1] which he summarizes as follows: "The model of behavior developed by modern society is characterized by empathy, a high capacity for rearranging the self-system on short notice. Whereas the isolate communities of traditional society functioned well on the basis of a highly constrictive personality, the interdependent sectors of modern society require widespread participation. This in turn requires an expansive and adaptive self-system, ready to incorporate new roles and to identify personal values with public issues. This is why modernization of any society has involved the great characterological transformation we call psychic mobility."[2] Or, even more naively expressed: "The media teach people participation...by depicting for them new and strange situations and by familiarizing them with a range of opinions among which they can choose. Some people learn better than others, the variation reflecting their differential skill in empathy... Empathy endows a person with the capacity to imagine himself as proprietor of a bigger grocery store in a city, to wear nice clothes and live in a nice house, to be interested in 'what is going on in the world' and to 'get out of his hole'. With the spread of curiosity and imagination among a previously quietistic population come the human skills needed for social growth and economic development."[3]

Defining "modernity" as "a participant style of life", Lerner is able to identify the personality transformation accompanying modernization (*qua* psychic mobility) as one of "empathy";[4] and to regard "media exposure", which is considered to increase empathy by giving it an opportunity to be exercised, as one of the

1. Daniel Lerner, *The Passing of Traditional Society: Modernizing the Middle East* (New York: Free Press, 1958), p. 77.
2. *Ibid.* p. 51.   3. *Ibid.* p. 412.
4. *Ibid.* p. 78. If traditional society and industrial society are opposed as a closed world to an open world, and if it can be assumed that to a more or less broad living space (real or imagined) there correspond different psychic dispositions, there nevertheless is no justification for privileging this opposition among a thousand other, equally pertinent ones.

decisive factors in attitude transformation.[5] There is no doubt that uprooting from the traditional order and an often brutal entry into the world of the modern economy bring about and presuppose systematic transformations of the habitus; but Lerner is taking the part for the whole and the effect for the cause when he reduces the process of adaptation to the modern economy to its psychological dimension alone, particularly when the variations observed in practices, dispositions, and opinions are attributed to a psychological disposition as ill-defined as empathy. In reality, "the characterological transformation[s] required by modernization",[6] like the "cultural transactions" that anthropologists talk about, are concretely accomplished by particular agents inserted in particular economic and social conditions – which is not to say that they owe nothing to the logic of acquired dispositions or of the cultural systems that are brought into contact.[7]

When he proceeds as if the adoption of a modern way of life were the result of a free choice, does not the sociologist reveal his implicit philosophy of history, in which "modern society", that is to say, American society in its capitalist form, is seen as the centre of a universal attraction? "Modernizing individuals", writes Lerner, "are considerably less unhappy – and the more rapidly the society around them is modernized the happier they are... Traditional society is passing from the Middle East because relatively few Middle Easterners *still want* to live by its rules."[8] Nietzsche might well have commented: "They would like, by every means, to convince themselves that the striving after *English* happiness, I mean after *comfort* and *fashion* (and in the highest instance, a seat

5. "Urban residence, schooling, media exposure...train and reinforce the empathic predisposition that was already present" (p. 60). "The importance of media exposure, in our theory, is that it enlarges a person's view of the world ('opinion range') by increasing his capacity to imagine himself in new and strange situations ('empathy')" (p. 96). "The male vanity culture which underlay Traditional institutions has proved relatively defenseless against the inroads of the mass media, particularly the movies" (p. 399).
6. *Ibid.* p. 76. The vocabulary Lerner uses ("characterological") is itself sufficient to indicate that he is implicitly referring to *natural* dispositions, although empathy is correlated with specifically sociological determinants such as education and town or country residence and, no doubt, occupation and social class.
7. Out of 117 questions, the questionnaire which serves as the basis for the "theory of modernization" has only 2 questions dealing with work and socio-economic position (as against 87 on the "mass media", the cinema, newspapers, radio, television); those variables are hardly ever taken into account in the analysis of the findings.
8. *Ibid.* pp. 398–9 (my italics).

in Parliament), is at the same time the true path of virtue; in fact, that in so far as there has been virtue in the world hitherto, it has just consisted in such a striving."⁹

In peasant society, the length of the farming cycles, which allowed effort, an "occasional cause", to be dissociated from its product, "the gift of God", the family solidarity which gave protection against absolute destitution, the reserves of food – all combined to veil the relationship between work and its product. In this economic universe, the transition from production activity oriented towards traditional goals to "rational" gainful activity is only accomplished slowly and progressively, because even when cash revenues have made their appearance alongside the customary resources, the produce of agriculture, husbandry, and family crafts enables at least a proportion of the group's needs to be satisfied without recourse to the market. In the urban world, on the other hand, the universalization of monetary exchanges, linked to the disappearance of other resources, makes obtaining a cash income an absolute, universal necessity.¹⁰ From the European farms in the Philippeville region where they used to go and work, the Kabyle peasants had brought back a saying which encapsulated their discovery of the modern significance of labour: "No work, no bread" (and also an expression: *achantyi ichumuran*, "unemployment site" (*chantier de chômage*)). To discover work as gainful activity – as opposed to traditional activity which now appears as merely keeping busy – is to discover its scarcity, a notion inconceivable in an economy which did not concern itself with productivity.

The pressure of the "industrial reserve army", always strongly felt, is sometimes expressed explicitly, whether in vague, general judgements ("There are a lot of arms", "There are too many people"), or in more concrete terms that are closer to a still vivid experience: "Go down to the waterfront one morning, and you'll see: there are hundreds, thousands of them, waiting for work, for a

9. *Beyond Good and Evil: Prelude to a Philosophy of the Future*, trans. H. Zimmern (Edinburgh: Foulis, 1909), p. 175.
10. The enforced regroupings of the population, which produced a quasi-urban situation in the Algerian countryside, brought about changes in economic attitude entirely analogous to those provoked by town-dwelling (see P. Bourdieu and A. Sayad, *Le déracinement: la crise de l'agriculture traditionelle en Algérie* (Paris: Editions de Minuit, 1964)).

day's work, to earn the bread to feed their kids" (labourer, Algiers). In such a context, competition for work is the primary form of the struggle for life, a struggle which, for some, begins anew every morning and has no more rules than a game of chance: "So there we are, waiting in front of a building site; it's like *qmar* [a game of chance]. Which one are they going to take?" (unemployed labourer, Constantine).

Competition is unrestrained because rational methods of recruitment cannot be applied to this army of equally defenceless labourers. For all those who have neither formal qualification nor special skill – the great majority – the freedom to choose their occupation is reduced to zero and their employment can only be the product of chance. Available for any job because really prepared for none, the unskilled, unqualified labourer is at the mercy of random hiring and lay-off. ("The labourer", said a shop worker, "is a Jack-of-all-trades – and master of none." And another: "He isn't a worker, he's a maid-of-all-work at the service of men.") "To each his luck", "To each his chance" – these stereotyped formulae translate the experience of the arbitrary decree which makes one man a worker and another unemployed. In the great majority of cases, the worker does not choose the job, the job chooses the worker. The young, forced to start earning their living very early, between ten and fifteen, are thrown into the competition for work without any preparation, when they are hardly out of school, if, that is, they have had the luck to go to school. The years of adolescence are the most difficult years of existence. This is the time of inevitable instability and makeshift jobs; before settling in regular employment, most permanent manual and clerical workers have had several successive jobs, which almost always means several bosses and often several trades.

We know that the earlier one leaves school, the narrower the range of choices. To each level of education corresponds a specific degree of freedom. In a society in which 87 per cent of the people have no certificate of general education and 98 per cent no certificate of technical education, possession of a trade proficiency diploma or a certificate of primary education give an enormous advantage in economic competition; a minute difference in level, such as that between someone who can read and someone who can read and also write, produces a quite disproportionate difference in chances of social success. Various consequences follow from this.

First, the barriers created by differences in schooling are very sharply defined, especially in the modern sector where advancement in the social hierarchy comes only by large leaps. Secondly, qualified and highly qualified workers enjoy an incomparable privilege: at a stroke they break away from the mass of people without any qualification and benefit from a whole range of safeguards, guarantees, and advantages. But the main beneficiaries of the "foil" effect of the general lack of qualification are those equipped with a certificate of general education who, by virtue of their small number, have no difficulty in monopolizing the administrative jobs and all the "noble" functions, the prestige attached to those functions redoubling the prestige traditionally accorded to the scholar. The life-style and the very existence of this sub-intelligentsia of minor bureaucrats – civil servants or clerks – who often use their competence as a charismatic technique, presuppose a largely illiterate society, uninformed about the structure of schooling and the hierarchies linked to it.

For the sub-proletarians, the whole of their working existence is dominated by arbitrariness. And indeed, in the absence of rational methods for matching workers and jobs and of any control of recruitment procedures, some employers may take advantage (or let advantage be taken) of the army of unskilled labourers who are prepared to accept any conditions in order to escape unemployment. In certain firms, especially in the construction industry, before a worker is taken on he has to pay baksheesh generally to the foreman. To force the hand of chance and overcome the hostility of an unjust order, those who have neither a "trade" nor "education" have another recourse, the power of patronage, "string-pulling", and "connections". Relations of kinship, neighbourhood, and comradeship tend to reduce the sense of arbitrariness but only by strengthening the – no less irrational – conviction that influence, connections, "smartness" (*chtara*), baksheesh, and "the café" can do everything. Doubtless, recourse to personal relationships is favoured by the whole cultural tradition which encourages and demands solidarity and mutual aid: the man who has succeeded must use his own success to help others, starting with the members of his own family; every self-respecting individual feels responsible for several more or less close relatives, for whom it is his duty, among other things, to find work by using his position and his personal connections. Nepotism is a virtue here.[11]

If the uncertainty of the recruitment procedures, the scarcity of skilled workers, and the surplus of manpower give strength to the belief in the omnipotence of influence, the effectiveness of patronage and connections is not the same throughout the different occupational categories and the different sectors of the economy. In the traditional sector, and particularly in the crafts and commerce, the old methods of recruitment still persist, especially in small family enterprises. Apart from all those who have inherited their workshop or store, a number of craftsmen and traders run a business owned by a relative; others have only been able to set up on their own account thanks to the financial aid of a relative or friend. In short, the traditional sector allows those who have no educational or technical assets to get round the barriers which rational or semi-rational rules of selection would put in their way. But in the modern sector itself, such rules often do not apply. It is not, strictly speaking, the firms that do the recruiting; new workers are taken on as a result of spontaneous co-option among those already there. And so, alongside the great occupational clans with their often long traditions – Mozabite shopkeepers, porters and greengrocers from the Djidjelli area, dustmen from Biskra (formerly water-carriers), waiters from the Michelet region, dishwashers from around Sidi-Aïch – there is a whole network of little groups, brought together by mutual aid or co-option, who maintain, in fragmented form, within the world of labour, a type of social relationship characteristic of a cultural system based on bonds of kinship and acquaintance.

The real value of connections is most manifest among clerical workers and supervisory staff. This is because, on the one hand, those who have had elementary education can expect to get one of the stable, less laborious, and hence supremely coveted jobs, such as that of orderly, or male nurse, so long as they have the support of a friend or relative; and on the other hand, sub-proletarians often have a less extensive and less strong network of social relations than regular workers, a handicap which is both the cause and a consequence of their relation to employment. For,

11. Mutual help is the only safety-net for the peasant who, in most cases, finds himself thrown abruptly into the city. The statistics show that, setting aside those who have been in a city for some time, more than two-thirds of the city-dwelling heads of families have come straight from the country, with no intermediate stage; only one-third of them have come via medium-sized towns. Everything seems to suggest that these two types of migration correspond to two different categories of the rural population. Those who migrate in great leaps seem to be predominantly the lower strata, regular or seasonal farm workers, *khammes* (sharecroppers), and smallholders, who take off aimlessly for the city or for France, expecting nothing better than a wage-earning job, or, if they cannot find one, then to set up as small traders. The short-range migrants seem to be more often medium landowners who move to the towns near their former residence, where they enjoy the advantages derived from their network of previous connections (e.g. credit), and where, thanks to the capital supplied by the sale of their land or its produce, they can find highly esteemed and less arduous trades such as commerce or traditional handicraft.

because of their instability, they have less chance of establishing connections, which are generally restricted to the place of work, than the long-standing employees of family business or the skilled workers attached to a firm.

When asked why their relationships are limited to their work place, they most often point out how arduous their task is and how far away they live. But what in fact seems to be determinant is their psychological distance from their work, the firm, and everything associated with it; a generalized refusal to adhere to a world that is hated as a whole; the desire to make as clear-cut a separation as possible between the work situation, where they feel inferior, and family life, which, to compensate, takes on a great importance. "I don't associate with anyone, I don't see anyone", said a driver, formerly a building labourer. "I go there, I come back; my family is all there is." And another worker said: "I haven't got any workmates; there are two of us cutters. When work is over, I go home: the kids are my pleasure" (cutter in a canvas factory, Oran). Poverty makes inroads into the traditions of mutual help, and some justify this renegation by pointing to the common destitution: "As we leave work I talk with them. We talk about our poverty and our worries and then everyone goes home because we're exhausted... There's no mutual help: we're all poor. For marriages and circumcisions and so on, you go and visit alone" (factory worker, Oran). Others take enforced individualism to its logical conclusion, forming all their relationships outside the world of work: "At work, every man for himself; after work, every man in his own home" (labourer, Oran). The establishment of friendly relations on the basis of work relations thus seems to be inseparable from a strong commitment to the trade and a strong integration into the working group. Skilled workers, who have generally been with their firms for a long time, are usually on good terms with their workmates. Only among some highly skilled workers does a new attitude appear: having succeeded in their working lives, they mean to keep aloof from the mass of unskilled workers and labourers, so that a narrowing circle of social relations is one of the indices of embourgeoisement.

Having been prepared by their whole cultural tradition to expect intense and overdetermined interpersonal relations, Algerian workers therefore tend to react with pain to the cold or brutal impersonality of work relations, perhaps especially in the case of relations with their superiors; but the fear of dismissal is such that the aspiration towards more human relations remains at the level of nostalgia. "I go in and put on my apron. 'Good morning, good morning; good night, good night', just like that, nothing more!" (The nostalgia for personal and symmetrical relationships is expressed through other indices: for example, the reason most often given by those who say they do not want to change their jobs so as to earn more money is their attachment to their bosses. Similarly, most workers and clerks in small businesses where patriarchal- or

Synoptic table of some of the statistical data used[a]

	Average number per family			Illiterate (%)	Speak correct French (%)	Wear European clothes (%)	String-pulling is all you need (%)	Dissatisfied with job (%)	Would change job for extra 5,000 francs (%)	Utopian hopes of better job (%)	Realistic hopes of better job (%)	Debts (%)	In favour of women working (%)
	Persons	Children	Economically active										
Sub-proletarians													
Unemployed and journeymen	5.7	2.6	0.40	81.2	12.5	43.8	83.3	100.0	86.2	51.8	0.0	34.4	15.6
Small traders	6.0	2.6	–	69.2	15.4	15.4	92.3	100.0	72.7	50.0	0.0	53.9	0.0
Labourers	6.2	3.2	*1.52*	71.4	50.0	71.4	85.7	100.0	100.0	38.4	7.6	71.4	15.4
Craftsmen and tradesmen	7.3	3.7	*1.48*[b]	65.0	30.0	45.0	52.6	90.0	50.0	50.0	0.0	45.0	15.0
Permanent skilled manual workers	6.4	3.0	1.05	48.3	75.9	86.3	67.8	75.8	41.3	20.7	58.7	20.6	39.3
Non-manual workers	6.1	3.0	1.36	0.0	*100.0*	83.3	41.6	66.5	41.6	8.3	75.1	41.7	27.3
Managerial staff in public and private sectors	7.2	2.8	*1.75*	0.0	*100.0*	83.3	41.6	33.5	18.1	33.3	66.1	16.7	36.3

[a] The italic figures indicate the two strongest tendencies in each column. The table is read thus: the unemployed and journeymen belong to families of, on the average, 5.7 persons, 2.6 children, and 0.4 economically active persons; 81.2 per cent of them are illiterate, 12.5 per cent speak correct French, 43.8 per cent wear European clothes, etc.
[b] Includes small traders.

paternalist-style working relations still survive say they like their jobs even when they are dissatisfied with their wages.) The younger workers, who have a more coherent political consciousness and more often arrive at the capitalist conception of labour as a mere means of acquiring a cash income, tend to consider their employers *as* employers and to adjust to neutral, impersonal relations, whereas the sub-proletarians most often express nostalgia for enchanted relationships or a Manichean antithesis between the bad foreman and the good boss.

Only in terms of a situation of chronic unemployment can it be understood why nearly three-quarters of those working say they dislike their trade; why the only reasons for dissatisfaction given are low wages and excessively arduous or dangerous work; why no one complains that he is deprived of initiative in his work and reduced to the role of executant; why low wages eclipse all other reasons for discontent, such as distance from home, the monotony of the task, ill-treatment or bullying by superiors (despite the fact that very many workers express their resentment of the contempt associated with degrading work); why only a few workers in the most favoured categories valorize the intrinsic interest of their task and expect it to make them rich or respected; why the aspiration towards more human relations in the place of work is expressed only in the form of resigned nostalgia or impotent revolt; why more than two-thirds of those who say they dislike their jobs also say they are not looking for another one; and why generalized discontent coincides with very great stability of employment.

> Conscious of the excess of manpower and knowing themselves to be as little irreplaceable as it possible to be, most labourers and office workers have no other concern than to keep their jobs, however detestable they may be. This is what emerges from the litany of reasons given by some to explain the failure of their search for something better, and by others to explain why they do not bother to search. "No, I haven't looked for anything else, because I wouldn't have found anything. I can't do anything else; to get work, you need education. Where can you find work nowadays? It's this job or nothing. Otherwise I starve." "I haven't got a trade, that's what my trade is." Forced adherence to a job to which no statable reason attaches them can only be understood in terms of the fear of unemployment. Their whole attitude towards their jobs is contained in the expression used by a labourer in Philippeville: "Of course, I have to like it [my work]. A starving man who finds a bone says, 'This is meat.'" Given the situation of structural unemployment, the fact of having a job, especially a regular one, rather than being unemployed cannot fail to be seen as a privilege.

The choice of instability is reserved for those whose qualification makes it certain that they will easily find a new job. For the rest, there is only forced instability and the fear of dismissal, which overcomes all other considerations. The most destitute often have to choose between hunger and contempt. So the demand for dignity, never absent, must give way to the imperative of work at any price. It comes to the foreground only for a minority of privileged individuals, freed from the fear of tomorrow, the petty bourgeoisie of junior and middle-rank civil servants.

Even if it is not clearly perceived as such, the most degrading work always remains something more and other than a way of earning a living, and unemployment is so intensely feared only because economic deprivation is accompanied by a social mutilation. So long as we think strictly in terms of economic profitability, how can we understand the behaviour of all the itinerant traders, sellers of trifles for trifling sums, who push their barrows around all day in the hope of selling a couple of water-melons, a second-hand garment, or a packet of peanuts? What, for those who do it and for their society, can be the function of this sort of work which ought rather to be called a way of being occupied?

First, the street hawker's activity is the only trade wich requires no initial capital, no professional qualification or special skill, no education, no money, no premises, no "connections". As such, it is the only resource of those who have nothing and for whom all occupations are closed, including, for lack of employers to hire them, the arduous and unanimously disparaged tasks of labouring "with pick and shovel". In general, the problem of the initial investment does not arise. It costs next to nothing to assemble the "equipment" – boxes mounted on bicycle wheels, prams with a wooden tray on top serving as a display, salvaged carts strung with cords on which to hang linen, secondhand clothes and trinkets, and innumerable other ingenious inventions. The goods are supplied by a relative or friend and paid back after they are sold. Behind the market brokers' backs, some of the wholesale greengrocers let relatives or friends from their region buy their vegetables cheap. But the itinerant trader's situation is not always so favourable: "Now I sell water-melons. Sometimes I stand in

The disenchantment of the world

the street all day without earning a penny... Today I've sold 80 francs' work of goods and I've been here all day. If I earned 50 francs a day, that would be all right. But unfortunately I'm not earning anything. There are days when the melons rot and I have to throw them away. I've got to buy a quintal of melons on credit. When I've sold the goods, I'll have to pay the wholesaler. Sometimes I give him everything and I'm left without a penny."

No doubt the income from such occupations, however derisory, is not negligible for those who have nothing. However, the proliferation of all these "pseudo-trades" cannot be explained simply in terms of interest and profit. The pressure of economic necessity and the situation of structural unemployment have the effect of perpetuating practices which borrow their justifications from the peasant morality of the past. In fact it is not uncommon to hear precepts stated which, on first analysis, appear to belong to the logic of the traditional ethos: "A worthy man, a man who doesn't want to live at others' expense, even if he has to live by his wits, must work. If he can't find any work, he can still be a street trader" (cook, Algiers) – in other words, in the language of the past, "he can carve his stick". And there is no doubt that, for those sub-proletarians in the towns who have kept a strong sense of dignity, the outward appearances of being occupied are the last resort against the ultimate degradation of the man who gets others to feed him, who lives at the expense of kinsmen or neighbours. Such activity has truly no other goal than to safeguard self-respect.

Does this mean that we should assign the same meaning and function to the symbolic activity of the urban sub-proletariat and to that of the old-fashioned peasant? Despite the apparent identity, traditional activity congruous with the expectations of the group differs both from labour *qua* productive activity and from merely being occupied. A society which, as peasant society does, accepts the duty of giving work to all its members and which, lacking the notion of productive or lucrative work and, by the same token, scarcity of work, has no place for the experience of unemployment, can consider that there is always something to be done by those who want to do something, and can treat work as a social duty, idleness as moral misconduct. Where activity is identified with social function and is not measured by the product in kind (still less in money) of the effort and time expended, everyone is entitled to feel and say he is busy, provided he fulfils the role appropriate to his age and status. In urban society, on the contrary, activity which does not procure a cash income is seen as bereft of what, in the new logic, is its natural result.

It is only because profitable work is closed to them that the sub-proletarians renounce economic satisfaction and fall back on occupations whose principal, if not exclusive, function is merely to provide a justification in the eyes of the group. Everything takes place as if they were forced by circumstances to dissociate work from its economic result, to understand it not so much in relation to its product as in opposition to non-work. To work, even for a minute income, means, both to oneself and to the group, that one is doing everything in one's power to earn a living by working, in order to escape the state of unemployment. Those who find themselves in a position where it is impossible to get real work endeavour to fill the abyss between their unrealizable aspirations and the effective possibilities by performing work whose function is doubly symbolic in that it gives a fictitious satisfaction to the man who performs it while at the same time providing him with a justification in the eyes of others, both those who depend on him and those to whom he must go for help in order to survive. The group, for its part, cannot reasonably hold the unemployed responsible for their lack of employment; but it is entitled to expect them to keep themselves occupied doing something. The logic of relationships between kinsmen never absolutely excludes self-interest and calculation; and so the duties of solidarity are only felt to be binding towards those whose attitude shows that they are the victims of an objective situation and not of their incapacity or laziness.

This being so, work in the sense of simply keeping busy can only be defined in negative terms. Awareness of the obstacles which stand in the way of getting a job would be regarded by everyone as an unanswerable excuse and would suffice to free the individual from his responsibility if people did not continue to believe that, ideally at least and in accordance with a different logic, the possibility always exists of doing something rather than nothing. But at the same time, everyone tends also to acknowledge that the only genuine work is work that brings in a cash income. This explains why, to justify activity undertaken for the sake of keeping busy, people should have recourse to ambiguous ideologies which mingle capitalist with pre-capitalist logic: "If he can't find work", said an informant, "he can sell things in the street." And the same respondent went on to say: "If work means having a trade, doing it regularly and earning a decent living...that's different. If work means doing something, doing anything at all rather than sit around doing nothing, so as to earn your daily bread, well, in that case only idlers don't work." So a man can simultaneously affirm the categorical duty of working, even for a virtually worthless product, and insist that that product, however derisory, is not negligible; whereas peasant society never dissociated the social function of activity from its economic function, here a distinction is made between the two functions, between work in the sense of productive, profitable activity and work as a way of fulfilling one's obligations towards the group.

The duality of the standards by which the fictitiously occupied sub-proletarians judge their own activity (and by which the group judges them) makes it into an ambiguous reality which, in order to be understood, requires that reference be made successively to two different grids. Thus activity as a mere state of being busy which abolishes any correspondence between income and labour time is totally absurd if one relates it solely to principles of economic rationality, and is reminiscent of the conduct of the old-style peasants which was based on the actual and essential incommensurability between the means employed and the purpose achieved and, more precisely, on the absence of any reckoning or quantification (by the expression of labour time in cash terms) of the expenditure of labour.

But, for the old-fashioned peasant, the absence of calculation and accounting is one of the constituent elements of the economic and social order to which he belongs. His economic activity, always charged with a plurality of unquantifiable, incommensurable functions, among which the economic function is never isolated and constituted as such, and employing means of various orders, themselves resistant to quantification and measurement, achieves traditional ends by traditional means. In contrast, even when necessity forces them to surrender their economic conduct and their whole existence to incoherence, the urban sub-proletarian and the proletarianized peasant always retain, from the economic system with which they have had to comply, the idea of calculability and even the capacity to comply with calculation, *in abstracto*. And so it is common for them to see their activity as devoid of profitability and consequently of meaning. "I'm in the shop all day", said a trader in Tlemcen, "from seven in the morning to eight in the evening. I just take Friday afternoon off. I know I don't sell anything. I sell just a little bit in the morning, when the women come out and do their shopping, but I stay there all the same, saying to myself, 'Perhaps there'll be a customer.' It's turning into a bad habit, and that's a fact. A bad habit! I arrive, I don't do any business, I just wait. But I have to be there. It's a bad habit! I don't make enough to feed my family."

In fact, whether they are seen as the pure product of necessity or as the consequence of strict obedience to the old logic, the new conducts are always accompanied by a certain number of ideologies which tend to rationalize the forced choices: the awareness that one can act differently is contained by the awareness of being prevented, in reality and by the weight of circumstances, from acting differently: "How could I not like my work?" "Who wouldn't want to get on in the world?" – questionings, heard a thousand times, all testifying to the fact that necessity can only appear as such to a consciousness for which other possibles exist.

Among all the workers who say they are prepared to work overtime, not one gives any other reason than the desire to earn more "so as to keep my family"; but there is no respondent who does not understand the meaning of the notion, at least sufficiently well to say that it has no meaning for a man who already works all day, which presupposes implicit reference to work limited in time and to the corresponding notion of an hourly wage. If most sub-proletarians identify the wage they consider they deserve with the income needed to satisfy their needs, if they are often indignant that remuneration is not defined in relation to the number of children, on the principle "To each according to his needs" and not "To each according to his deserts", and if they rarely bring the notion of the hourly wage into their assessments, nonetheless they cannot ignore the demands the new system makes of them, even when it prohibits them from fulfilling those demands.¹²

With economic necessity tending to require the subordination of all the ends (particularly the traditional ones) and all the means of activity to the monetary product, the old norms and especially those which regulated relations with kinsmen, as well as the old values of honour and solidarity, must also reckon with the demands of calculation and sometimes give way to them. In southern Algeria, where the traditional economy has remained relatively intact, the head of the family (that is to say, for the purposes of the survey, the person who states that he is the head of the family) is generally the oldest member. His authority rests on the traditional foundations and is quite independent of his contribution to the economic life of the group, the other members of the family remaining in a relation of dependence, whatever their effective contributions. Undivided ownership ensures the patriarchal authority which in turn guarantees the unity of the undivided fmaily. In general, and although it is becoming rarer, undivided ownership is more readily accepted in rural areas, because the monetary outlook has not made such inroads and the corresponding attitudes are less widespread, but also and especially because the major resource remains the direct product of agriculture. In regions where the capitalist economy has made greater inroads, in Kabylia for example, and *a fortiori* in the cities, increasingly it is the man who makes the greatest contribution to the family budget who declares himself head of the family, regardless of his age. However, there are qualifications to be made. When the father works, like his son, and is still relatively young, he may retain effective authority; so may the elder brother. Most often a sort of division of powers takes place spontaneously, the young head of the household tending to take the decisions that concern the family's economic life and all its relations with the modern economic world to which he is objectively better adapted, often because he has had more education. In short, analysis of concrete situations brings out a whole range of forms of possible

12. A number of respondents assess their own situation by comparison with that of civil servants: "If I worked for the government, I'd have regular working hours and I could take leave" (head of a dairy, Algiers). "I can't do overtime, my work isn't limited...A shopkeeper doesn't work fixed hours; I'm talking about this firm" (cloth merchant's clerk, Tlemcen).

relations, from maintenance of patriarchal authority to complete reversal of the customary relationship.

A first consequence follows: the advent of a plurality of money incomes, measurable and commensurable, contains the potentiality of a breakup of undivided ownership and threatens the authority of the head of the family, since the economic dependence of the other members steadily diminishes and each of them can demand his share of the total income. For once the respective contributions are made in the form of cash, rational accountancy becomes possible and each individual or each household can evaluate precisely its share in income and expenditure. This means the end of the "repression" of calculation which was permitted by undivided possession and which in turn safeguarded undivided possession: "At home", said a labourer, "there are four brothers and two sisters with their husbands. In all there are twenty-eight children. There are forty-eight of us all together. We've stopped sharing the same cooking-pot because the women used to say, 'My kid hasn't got enough to eat.' There were arguments all the time. Now my mother eats with me, the eldest son." The breakup of the extended family is both the precondition for the rationalization of the domestic economy and of economic conduct in general, and also the product of that rationalization, as is shown by the fact that the married couple tends to become the basic economic and social unit as the degree of adaptation to the economic system increases and incomes rise. This breakup is held back by the housing shortage, which keeps together households which are destined to go their separate ways as they have the opportunity. Though cohabitation stands in the way of the rationalization of conduct, because, like undivided possession, it rules out long-term undertakings and keeps families in forced incoherence by preventing calculation, it enables the poorest to achieve a form of equilibrium, on account of the plurality of (simultaneous or successive) sources of income as against a single outlet for expenditure: "My father was a shopkeeper", said a cloth merchant in Tlemcen, "and he persuaded me to buy a business with him. He's old now, but he still has his business and he works. He's the one who keeps the family alive; I've got three children and I haven't got enough money. I couldn't live on what I earn and he's the one who helps us... I'd need three or four thousand francs a day to live without my father's help, if I was alone with my wife and kids."

In addition to the increased autonomy of the couple, which tends to become an independent economic unit and even to break away whenever its resources permit, the change in the structure of the activities of the different members of the family produces a certain number of important transformations. First, even when urbanization brings about emancipation in other areas, the wife's economic dependence increases, especially since even partial or unconscious adoption of capitalist economic dispositions leads people to disparage female activities by acknowledging as real work only that which brings in a money income. Unable to take outside work, the wife is assigned to the home and is completely excluded (except in the most privileged strata) from the important economic decisions, sometimes not even knowing how much her husband earns. So long as the ideology which could justify and valorize her new function remains unformed, she finds herself relegated to an inferior rank and role more brutally and more totally than before, because the new economic and social universe tends to dispossess her even from the functions which the old society acknowledged to be hers.

On the other hand, although the chronic underemployment tends to pull in the opposite direction, the dependence of the young on their parents decreases as soon as they start bringing in a salary, especially when their schooling has made them more adapted to the economic world. Thus, whereas in the traditional society they remained dependent on their father so long as he was alive, urban society sometimes provides them with the economic conditions for emancipation. Conscious of bringing in a share of the family income, they seek to participate in the management of the budget even when, as often happens, they still hand over all or part of their wages to their fathers. Every family is the site of a clash of civilizations. However, the tension between the generations (which is often made more complex when three ages cohabit) does not always take an acute form, whether because the son, more respectful of tradition, agrees to hand over all his earnings without counting, as is frequently the case in crafts or commerce; or because the households separate, to the great indignation of the parents; or because, as increasingly happens, the father decides to accept the new model of relations between parents and children and also the corresponding ideology; or because, as an extreme solution, the father or elder brother pays a wage to the son or younger brother.

The young are emancipated that much earlier the sooner they find regular, well-paid employment and the better educated they are, or, more exactly, the greater the difference in level between parents and children. The extreme case is that of families in which the uneducated father has to ask his son or daughter to read or compose his letters, fill in administrative forms, and even guide his decisions concerning the family's economic life. More commonly, the father, as exemplified by a craftsman in Tlemcen, maintains an absolute authority over the older, uneducated sons and allows almost total freedom to the younger ones who go to school. The fact remains that in most cases the undisputed authority of the head of the family, who decided and ordered everything, is gone for good. Those who are most attached to the old order have to accommodate themselves to the new values which have come in irresistibly with the generalization of monetary exchanges, independently of the influence exerted by the example of the family life of the Europeans. The dispositions which are bound up with the modern economy, in the forefront of which stand the pursuit of profit and the spirit of calculation, are indeed the very antithesis of those which safeguarded the traditional family: whereas in the old society economic relations were conceived on the model of kinship relations, now kinship relations themselves are not exempt from economic calculation.

With growing adaptation to the capitalist economy and growing assimilation of the corresponding dispositions comes increasing tension between the traditional norms which impose duties of solidarity towards the extended family and the imperatives of an individualistic, calculating economy. The sub-proletarians are subjected to contradictory pressures which give rise to ambiguous attitudes: thus the necessities of the economy can develop in them the spirit of calculation which economic necessity prevents them from exercising in their daily conduct. More precisely, the spirit of calculation which enters, as we have seen, with calculability (that is, concretely, with monetary incomes) contradicts the old type of family relationship just at the time when economic constraints and

The disenchantment of the world

the housing shortage often demand the maintenance or reconstitution of the extended families. Undivided ownership in the shanty towns is closer to what the Kabyles call "sharing-out indoors" than to the arrangement which supplied the cohesion of the old extended family: just as, for the sake of honour, some families abandon common ownership internally and secretly share out all the goods while maintaining the fiction of unity for external purposes, so urban families often present only a facade of joint ownership, because the spirit of calculation is gnawing away at a unity imposed by necessity.

Thus economic necessity can lead the most underprivileged to behave in ways which can be seen either as the fulfilment or as the betrayal of the tradition. Such conduct assumes its full meaning neither in terms of the traditional logic nor in terms of the logic of the capitalist economy. In reality, like an ambiguous *Gestalt*, each practice lends itself to a dual reading because it contains reference to the two logics imposed by necessity. Thus the hand-to-mouth existence of the sub-proletarian or the proletarianized peasant differs totally from the security-encircled existence of the old-style fellah. In one case, the search for subsistence is the sole and unanimously approved goal guaranteed by the rules of custom; in the other case, getting the minimum required for survival is the goal imposed by necessity on an exploited class. Because the context has changed and everybody is aware of it, because the economic assurances and psychological security that were previously given by an integrated society and a living tradition have been swept away, hazardous improvisation has to take the place of customary foresight and the reassuring stereotyping of behaviour. Thus unemployment and intermittent employment produce a disorganization of conduct which it would be a mistake to see as innovation based on a conversion of outlook. The traditionalism of despair and the absence of a life-plan are two faces of the same reality.

3 ❦ Subjective hopes and objective chances

To tear oneself from the world in order to confront or master it is to tear oneself from the immediate present and the imminent "forthcoming", an urgency and threat with which the present is fraught. The sub-proletarian, locked in the present, knows only the free-floating indefinite future of his daydreams. Because the field of possibles has the same limits as the field of objective possibilities, the individual project and the revolutionary consciousness are closely allied. Before individual practices – not least, economic acts – can be organized in accordance with a life-plan and before a systematic, rational awareness of the economic system *as* a system can be formed, there has to be some relaxation in the pressure of the economic necessity which forbids that suspension of fascinated adherence to the present "given" without which no "lateral possible" can be posited. It follows that to the different stages of the process leading from existence abandoned to chance to economic conduct regulated by calculation, correspond different forms of awareness of unemployment and of revolutionary consciousness.[1]

When asked what income they would need in order to live well, the individuals with the smallest resources tend on the whole to formulate inordinate aspirations which seem to be randomly distributed, the disparity between the income considered necessary and their real income being in most cases enormous. Everything takes place as if most sub-proletarians were incapable of measuring their needs, even in the mode of abstract calculation. And yet, because it belongs among the most everyday and most pressing preoccupations, estimation of needs is less likely to get detached

---

1. In order to bring out more clearly the structural affinity between political dispositions and economic dispositions, I have presented in a synoptic and schematic form the description of the different systems of dispositions to which I return below.

from the real than opinions concerning aspects of existence about which, as one interviewee said, "you have the right to dream". So if we must hierarchize opinions involving the future according to their modality, from the daydream to the project rooted in present conduct, we must not forget that the degree of commitment in the opinion formulated varies with the degree of accessibility of the future that is aimed at. Now, this future is more or less accessible depending on the material conditions of existence and social status of each individual and also on the area of existence that is at stake: thus opinions concerning the children's future are even more vague than the estimation of needs, because the former presuppose a life-plan stretching over two generations.

It is not surprising to find that aspirations tend to become more realistic, more strictly tailored to the real possibilities, in proportion as the real possibilities become greater. So it is that the disparity between the income estimated to be necessary and the present income decreases as real income increases, which indicates that the distance between the standard aspired to and the real standard of living, between needs and means, tends to fall as income rises and as economic calculation comes to be embodied in conduct.

The field of the real "forthcoming", that is, of the really accessible future, which is extremely limited for the sub-proletarians condemned to project impossible possibles, is steadily enlarged. The degree of freedom conferred on each worker, the freedom to choose his job and his employer, the freedom to define the rhythm and quality of his work, the freedom to demand respect in work relationships, varies considerably according to socio-occupational category, income, and especially the degree of skill and level of education. Similarly, the field of possibles tends to expand as one rises in the social hierarchy: whereas the great majority cannot expect either length of service or wage demands to bring about a better occupational situation and higher social status, a privileged minority enjoys a whole set of assurances concerning the present and the future. Like social ascent in the course of a lifetime, mobility over two generations, which is always relatively rare, varies considerably among the different categories.[2]

2. For the sons of smallholders or farm workers, social ascent, which is always very rare, entails a break with the family milieu through emigration to the towns or to France. For the sons of tradesmen and craftsmen, the chances of social mobility are inversely

Whether the respondent is estimating the needs of his family or considering the future of his children – who are seen as a liability as soon as attention is seriously given to their future and particularly their education – whether he is envisaging his own occupational future or passing general judgements on society as a whole, the opinions expressed are more realistic, that is, more closely adjusted to reality, and more rational, that is, more strictly subjected to calculation, the higher the effective possibilities (for which level of education and income are good indices). The expectation of rising in one's trade varies significantly according to socio-occupational category, as does the modality of that hope. The instability of employment and the consequent irregularity of income, the lack of assurances concerning even the immediate future, the awareness (aggravated by experience) of completely lacking the means needed in order to escape from incoherence and contingencies, condemn the sub-proletarians to despair. When they are asked about their hopes of rising in their occupations, they often reply with a joke: "I don't hope for anything", said a Saïda roadmender; "I'm a pick and shovel man." They are denied not only all reasonable hope of rising in society but even the very idea of such a hope: "I work all year round for 9,000 francs a fortnight plus 2,000 a month. That makes 20,000. With nine mouths to feed, how do you expect me to live on that? I have to push the cars, we're not allowed to start them. I look after them. I've been doing the same every day for a long time. Get on in the world? Are you dreaming or do you want me to dream? I haven't got a trade and I'll never learn one doing what I do now. Now, if I'd had some education I could've found another job. I could have had some hope..." (garage watchman, Philippeville). In the absence of reasonable expectations, all that is left is daydream and utopia. The gap between aspirations and reality tends towards infinity. If the realistic hope of higher status always becomes more frequent as income increases, it seems to depend more precisely on the guarantees and assurances about the future given by the occupation one is in. A study of the modality of the hopes of social ascent over two generations, as expressed in the wishes formulated

related to the size of the business, the strength of the trade traditions and the likelihood of coming into a large inheritance. The very small tradesmen are the ones who provide a relatively large contingent of industrial and office workers.

The disenchantment of the world

for the children's future, confirms the previous analyses. Outlooks on the future depend closely on the objective potentialities which are defined for each individual by his or her social status and material conditions of existence. The most individual project is never anything other than an aspect of the subjective expectations that are attached to that agent's class.

It is clearly among the sub-proletarians that the abyss between the imaginary and experience is greatest and incoherence between opinions most frequent. An unemployed man in Constantine, completely without resources, estimates that he would need 200,000 francs a month to satisfy his family's needs. Asked what future he would like for his children, he says: "They would go to school; when they had got enough education they would choose for themselves. But I can't send them to school. If I were able to, I'd like to keep them at school long enough to become doctors or lawyers. But there's no one to help me. I've got the right to dream dreams!" We find the same disconnection between imaginary aspirations and the real situation in the words of the unemployed man in Saïda who, after saying he fears he will have to take his children away from school for lack of money, says he hopes his daughter will "carry on with her education right the way through, until she's succeeded. Up to the *baccalauréat*, if she can, or up to the *brevet*. That way she can work as a schoolteacher." These are the same people who, asked whether they want their children to carry on their studies after the primary school certificate, often reply, "Yes, right the way through", or, like a labourer in Oran, "Put down whatever is best." The same unqualified affirmation, the same dreamlike absence of realism, are expressed in their answers concerning women's employment. It is in fact always the persons with the lowest incomes who provide the highest rate of black-and-white responses, whether positive or negative.

With regular wage-earners one enters another world. Awareness of limits is expressed at the same time as the realistic hope of advancement: "I'd like to be an assistant orderly", said a ward boy at Constantine hospital. "You need qualifications to be an orderly. You can't get something just by asking for it. You need to take lessons. A man who's an assistant orderly – and you can do it with a primary education certificate – can really earn something. With the family allowances, he can make 10,500 francs." Asked about his children's future, he replies: "That's a difficult one. I haven't been able to think about it yet. A technical trade – engineer, technician. There are too many doctors. What we need is engineers. If there are ten cafés, you don't set up in the café business. There are doctors who are unemployed. If I make my children engineers, it's so they'll be looked up to." This example will suffice to show how aspirations tend to be circumscribed as the possibility of satisfying them increases, perhaps because there is a sharper awareness of the difficulties in the way, as if nothing were really impossible so long as nothing is really possible.

In short, the whole range of economic attitudes is defined in relation to two thresholds. Permanent employment and regular income, together with the whole set of assurances about the future which they guarantee, bring people on to what we may call the *security plateau*: the goal of economic activity remains the satisfaction of needs, and behaviour obeys the principle of maximum security. Arrival at the *threshold of calculability* (or enterprise), which is essentially marked by possession of incomes sufficient to overcome the concern with simple subsistence, coincides with a profound change in dispositions: the rationalization of conduct tends to extend to the domestic economy, the site of the last resistances, and at this point the agents' dispositions form a system organized by reference to a future that is grasped and mastered by calculation and forecast. Thus, of the many indices of the transformation of the economic habitus in response to new conditions of existence, perhaps one of the most reliable is the number of persons employed in each family, since, among the means of increasing income, multiplication of the sources of income by sending several family members to work serves the same function for the most disadvantaged categories as overtime or promotion for the others. The mean percentage of economically active persons per family, highest in the lowest income bracket, steadily decreases with increased family income and then steadily rises again, suggesting that beyond the security plateau the multiplication of sources of income becomes an imperative. As soon as permanent employment appears on the scene, supplementary resources, often derived from improvised sidelines, lose their significance, now that security is ensured. At the higher threshold one sees the reappearance of multiple jobs, but all of them regular and well paid.

It goes without saying that this model is only valid for workers in the modern sector. Shopkeeping and handicrafts constitute a protected, reserved island offering a refuge for those who are not armed for economic competition at the same time as it holds back in a pre-capitalist logic capitals and capacities which could be invested in the modern sector.

Algerian capital tends to be invested in commerce or in those sectors of industry (textiles, clothing, leather and furs, food) in which traditional, family-type firms can be kept up, often run like commercial or money-lending businesses, with the owner taking charge of the financial management, personally buying the raw material, deciding the prices, and overseeing sales. Like industries of this type, commerce requires no complex technical competences, and it is even possible to delegate the day-to-day running of the firm to a relative. Furthermore, it is certain that capital invested by a tradesman yields a return much sooner than capital invested in manufacturing industry. The retailer and the middleman who can conduct their business without acquiring property rights over the commodities being marketed run the minimum of risks, since, apart from the losses due to deterioration of the goods, the most they can lose is the resale profit. The industrial entrepreneur who invests more capital and for a longer period has to reckon with the changing economic situation, and in particular, because he cannot take in the whole production process at a glance, he has to resort to rational calculation of the risks and likelihoods. The attitude to time and to calculation that shopkeeping authorizes is what makes it the refuge of the pre-capitalist spirit within the urban world and what causes the small shopkeeper to resemble the small peasant in so many features of his life-style and world-view.

These activities, which are generally expected to provide nothing more than the means of subsistence, are seen as a second best even by those who practise them. The competition of European commerce and of the rationalized section of Algerian commerce (e.g. the Mozabite firms in Algiers and a number of other Algerian towns) condemns the small tradesmen to the most impoverished clientele, who will patronize their shops so long as they give credit and discounts. Low and unreliable profits, little capital – and that often tied up in the form of loans to customers – these are objective obstacles to rationalization. Moreover, often perpetuating countrymen's attitudes in the urban world, the shopkeepers are generally reluctant to rationalize their businesses. Most are illiterate, know nothing of double-entry bookkeeping or the distinction between the family budget and the business budget, and often confuse takings with profits; a long series of infinitesimal transitions leads from very small-scale trading as a mere way of keeping busy to really profitable commerce. It is not surprising that handicrafts and shopkeeping should be the refuge for traditionalism in urban society: there is nothing in his occupational activity, his work environment (most often merged with the family home), or his contacts with his customers that can provoke the shopkeeper to change his style and habits of thinking; on the contrary, the system of representations and values handed down by tradition is perfectly consistent with an economic activity that excludes rationalization.

The construction of a coherent picture of the social world and of the agent's position in that world is subject to the same conditions as the construction of a life-plan. The awakening of class consciousness, in the sense of a taking hold of the objective truth of one's own position in the production relations and of the social mechanisms producing and tending to reproduce that position, is not independent of the agent's position in those relations and of the action of the mechanisms which determine it. In short, there are economic conditions for the awareness of economic conditions. The more individuals who were questioned about the causes of unemployment, the more forms and degrees one recorded of consciousness of the same situation, apprehended through different experiences.[3] From pure and simple surrender up to coherent totalization runs a whole series of gradations. "There's unemployment" or "There's too much unemployment", "There's no work" or "not enough work", "There are lots of people" or "too many people": such statements, however rudimentary, are only apparently self-evident. Unemployment haunts these people's thinking. It governs their conduct, orients their opinions, inspires their emotions. And yet it often escapes explicit consciousness and systematic statement. It is the invisible centre

3. The decision to question respondents about the causes of unemployment as a way of grasping their political attitudes was a necessary one in view of the police activities which ruled out any direct questioning on the revolutionary war. But it was also motivated by the aim of encountering those attitudes on the terrain on which they were most likely to be expressed with the maximum of realism. In reality, as was shown even by the analysis of the responses (especially statistical analysis of the variations in the implicit definition of work and unemployment entailed by stating whether or not one was head of the family), the mere fact of talking about unemployment virtually imposed a problematic (especially when the question was put to the least urbanized and the oldest respondents).

around which behaviour revolves, the virtual vanishing point of the sub-proletarian world-view.

If awareness of unemployment can exist without being formulated except in the language of practices or in a discourse which is a tautology for the real, it can also, as we have seen, be totally absent; for, so long as labour is defined as social function, the notions of unemployment or underemployment cannot take shape. The emergence of awareness of unemployment thus marks a conversion of people's attitude to the world. Natural adhesion to an order regarded as natural, because traditional, is henceforward suspended; customary work is conceived and measured in terms of a new system of reference – the notion of full employment that is derived from experience of work in the modern sector. So it is that, at very similar levels of activity, country-dwellers in the Kabyle regions readily state themselves to be unemployed if they consider that they are insufficiently occupied, whereas the farmers and shepherds of south Algeria tend to say that they are "kept busy". It is equally possible to say that the Kabyle unemployed are farmers who describe themselves as unemployed or that the south Algerian farmers are unemployed but unaware of it. The Kabyles, former emigrants or members of a group whose economic practices and conceptions of the economy have been profoundly altered by a long tradition of emigration to the towns of Algeria or to France, conceive traditional farming activity in terms of the sole activity worthy of the name, the work that brings in money; and so they can only see it as unemployment. The southerners, in the absence of such a conception of work, cannot see as unemployment the inactivity to which they are condemned, still less the ways of keeping busy that the traditional order allots to them.

Thus unemployment can first exist "in itself", without being grasped *as* unemployment; at a second level, "consciousness" of unemployment can manifest itself in practice without becoming explicit, or becoming so only in very rudimentary forms of discourse such as the pleonastic statement of the given. The expression of consciousness of unemployment therefore marks the transition to a third level. From this point on, consciousness and its expression come hand in hand; the wealth and clarity of the content of consciousness grow at the same time as the wealth and clarity of the expression it receives. A large number of interviewees put forward partial explanations which are most often nothing other than the statement of the most strongly felt experiences of their occupational lives; their explanations always bear the mark of the circumstances and concrete conditions of their emergence. Others, a minority, offer a mass of one-sided explanations, simply juxtaposed in an aggregate; all concern to synthesize is generally absent, as is shown by their contradictions and the fact that it is often hard to distinguish between incomplete expression and stereotype.[4]

We must set apart what might be called affective quasi-systematization, that is to say, a unitary outlook on the economic and social world whose unifying principle is not of the order of the concept but of emotion, and which perceives the colonial world as a universe dominated by a malignant, all-powerful will. For what is practically given in daily experience is concrete inequalities and particular conflicts; the colonial system is grasped only through its manifestations. And so the structure and objective mechanisms of the system, above all the system as such, are bound to escape the grasp of minds absorbed in the immediate difficulties of daily life: revolt is primarily directed against individual persons or situations, never against a system requiring systematic transformation. And how could things be otherwise? What is perceived is not discrimination but the racialist; not exploitation but the exploiter; not even the boss, but the Spanish foreman.

Closely bound to a particular situation, the sub-proletarians are unable to go beyond the phenomenal manifestations of the colonial system which stop them and where they themselves stop because those manifestations present themselves with exceptional urgency in their daily existence and are charged with emotional power. When asked to give reasons for a world which defies reason, they can only fall back on stereotypes, a language halfway between fiction and experience, between the constructed and the accidental, which seems to refer to the given when it is entirely imaginary and which appears as *flatus vocis* even when it expresses experience, because the automatic interlocking of words stands in for authentic meanings.

4. Here are two examples of these two categories of responses:
    A. "There aren't enough factories" or "There isn't any work because there are too many foreigners."
    B. "There aren't enough factories: the Spaniards take all the jobs and there's nothing left for us, so what do you expect?"

It is among the sub-proletarians and also the petty bourgeois that one encounters the highest proportion of stereotyped remarks and of speech obeying the logic of affective quasi-systematization. Empty words are not peculiar to the sub-proletarians. However, whereas among the petty bourgeois empty speech often only expresses disarmed pretension, in the mouths of the sub-proletarians it always retains a sort of truth and plenitude because, like a cry, it expresses dramatically a dramatic experience and presents itself neither as a sufficient explanation of an inexplicable existence nor as an adequate expression of an inexpressible experience, but as an incoherent confession of an insuperable incoherence.

However, the systematic character of the most diverse experiences, from victimization to unemployment, is felt vividly. And so the simple description of a particular datum, a certain type of interpersonal relationship for example, overflows towards a grasp of the system that is external and superior to individuals. "The European is favoured here. For us, unemployment is something natural. For a European, it's a scandal no one can tolerate – the authorities couldn't, nor could other Europeans. Every effort is made to find something for him. They discover he has skills and qualifications; even if he hasn't got any, they find some. And once he's been put in a job, he always turns out to be at least a little bit higher placed than all the Muslims. He can't be a worse workman than they are! That's what string-pulling can do, and yet you never know who pulled the string: everyone did" (cabinet-maker, Algiers). Thus, particular experiences can be understood, by those who experience them, as the outcome of a sort of systematic plan. For indeed, within this logic, only a will can be responsible for the coherent and quasi-methodical character of the trials that are undergone, and only a diabolical will could so ingeniously contrive to entrap men in an irresistible chain of catastrophic situations.

Unemployment is understood not as an aspect of an economic and social conjuncture but as the work of a sort of evil hidden god who may be embodied, depending on the occasion, in "the Europeans", "the Spaniards", "the French", "the authorities", "the Government", "Them", or "Other people", and who wills that of which it is said "thus it is willed". "The French", said an unemployed man in Saïda, "don't want to give me any work. All these gentlemen around me have no work. They've all got certificates. One is a mason, another a driver, they've all got a trade. So why haven't they got a right to work? We are short of everything; the French have everything they need to live well. But they don't want to give us anything – neither work nor anything else." And a grocer in Algiers: "Those who have work to give should give it, and not hide it." The frequency and emotional intensity with which "string-pulling" (*le piston*) is referred to, always in the vaguest possible terms, sometimes without any reference to a situation concretely experienced, shows clearly that, for the most underprivileged, it is a datum of mythic reason as much as of experience. The living of life as a game of chance conjures up powers, impersonal and personalized, omnipresent and localized, beneficent and maleficent, which impel and animate the whole social universe. "Nowadays", said an Oran street porter, "everything makes way for *le piston*! That's the way it is! Hard work gets you nowhere. But *le piston* always does the trick!" The malignant *piston* and its manifestations, discrimination, the colonists, the Spaniards, or the machines, all these hostile powers, springing from experience, are transfigured by mythic reason. And the sense of systematic malevolence combines naturally with belief in the omnipotence of the benignant *piston*, the *baraka* of the sub-proletarian.

Pessimistic fatalism, based on the conviction that it is absurd to struggle against an all-powerful evil, owes nothing to the feeling of *mektub* in old religiosity. The revolt of resentment, which attacks not so much the system as such as its manifestations, is generally only an aspect of resigned surrender, and miserabilism draws on the same logic as emotional quasi-systematization. Those who say "They don't want to give us work" are also those who say "They don't give us enough." By substituting intention for necessity, people put themselves at the mercy of the arbitrary decrees of the power of which they are the victims, but from which they expect, by way of alms, in spite of everything, the satisfaction of their vital aspirations. Is this not the deep significance of the conduct of the candidates for employment who persist in aiming at the impossible, as if to mask or offset, with displaced ambitions, a defeat or surrender that has already been unconsciously recognized?

Affective quasi-systematization typifies the understanding the sub-proletarian makes for himself of the economic and social world. Emotion is indeed the only possible basis for unifying a dramatic experience dominated by incoherence. The sufferings imposed by the most inhuman situation are not sufficient motives for conceiving a new economic and social order. On the contrary, everything takes place as if poverty had to be eased, so making it possible to conceive a different economic and social order, before poverty itself can be grasped as such and imputed to a system that is explicitly grasped as unjust and unacceptable. Because poverty imposes itself on them with a necessity so total that it allows them no glimpse of a reasonable exit, sub-proletarians tend to live their suffering as habitual and even natural, as an inevitable ingredient in their existence; and because they do not possess the indispensable minimum of security and culture, they cannot clearly conceive the total change in the social order which could abolish the causes of their suffering. After showing me his wretched dwelling and pointing to the destitution of his children, a driver in Oran added: "That's what my life is. The only thing wrong is the wages. As for the rest, we're made for that."

Because their awareness of the objective barriers to getting a job or adequate wages brings them back to their awareness of their incapacities, their lack of education or occupational skill for example, the sub-proletarians tend to attribute their inadequacies to the inadequacies of their own being rather than to the inadequacies of the objective order. ("To each his own fortune", said a Constantine labourer. "A man who isn't educated has nothing. They make him toil until he drops. That's the life of a man who can't read.") They can never attain an awareness of the system as being *also* responsible for their lack of education or occupational skill, that is, both for their inadequacies and for the inadequacies of their being.

Far from being intrinsically capable of determining an apprehension of the given as intolerable or revolting, the pressure of economic necessity even tends to prohibit the awakening of consciousness, which presupposes something very different from a sort of revolutionary *cogito*. Failing to grasp their own situation as one aspect of a whole system, the sub-proletarians cannot link the betterment of their condition to a radical transformation of the system: their aspirations, their demands, and even their revolt are expressed within the logic the system imposes on them. Thus "string-pulling", a product of the system, is seen as the only way of inflecting the systematic rigour of the system. In short, absolute alienation annhilates even awareness of being alienated.

Before the awareness of unemployment and of the system creating it can be stated, the urgency of the world has to be relaxed: consciousness of the absence of work and of its objective basis is different from, and of another order than, the implicit knowledge which is only expressed in practice or in the ambiguous and often contradictory language of feeling. On the one hand, there is the revolt of emotion, the uncertain and incoherent expression of a condition characterized by uncertainty and incoherence; on the other hand, there is revolutionary radicalism, springing from the systematic consideration of reality. These two attitudes correspond to two types of material conditions of existence: on the one hand, the sub-proletarians of the towns and the uprooted peasants whose whole existence is constraint and arbitrariness; on the other hand, the regular workers of the modern sector, provided with the minimum of security and guarantees which allow aspirations and opinions to be put in perspective. Disorganization of daily conduct prohibits the formation of the system of rational projects and forecasts of which the revolutionary consciousness is one aspect. A *force for revolution*, the proletarianized peasantry and the urban sub-proletariat do not constitute a *revolutionary force* in the true sense. With permanent employment and regular wages, an open and rational temporal consciousness is able to be formed; actions, judgements, and aspirations can be ordered in relation to a life-plan. Then, and then only, does the revolutionary attitude take the place of escape into daydreams or fatalistic resignation.

This is why we must challenge the thesis that, in the colonized countries, the proletariat is not a true revolutionary force, since, unlike the peasant masses, it has everything to lose, having become an irreplaceable cog in the colonial machine. It is true that, in a society haunted by unemployment, those workers who are sure of a permanent job and a regular income form a privileged category. It is true that, *always and everywhere*, the proletariat is determined, as much as by its material conditions of existence, by the *position* it occupies in the social structure, not at the very bottom, in the abyss, as a certain eschatological vision of revolution as a reversal would have it, but at the peak of a *negative career*, the one which leads towards a relapse into the sub-proletariat. More simply, it would be easier to understand practices too readily imputed to the conservatism of proletarians (or of their "apparatuses") if it

The disenchantment of the world

were realized that, like the effective solidarity it gives, the slim advantages associated with stability of employment are at the mercy of accident, illness, and lay-offs, and that all that bourgeois commentators (revolutionary or not) are quick to describe as signs of embourgeoisement are first of all bulwarks raised against the counter-attacks of poverty.

To those who have the "privilege" of undergoing permanent and "rational" exploitation and of enjoying the corresponding advantages also belongs the privilege of a truly revolutionary consciousness. This realistic aiming at the future (*l'avenir*) is only accessible to those who have the means to confront the present and to look for ways of beginning to implement their hopes, instead of giving way to resigned surrender or to the magical impatience of those who are too crushed by the present to be able to look to anything other than a utopian future (*un futur*), an immediate, magical negation of the present.

4 ❧ The economic conditions for transformed economic dispositions

Economic and political dispositions can only be understood by reference to the economic and social situation which structures the agents' whole experience through the mediation of their subjective apprehension of their objective, collective future. That apprehension derives its form, modality, and content from the potentialities objectively inscribed in the situation, that is, from the future (*l'avenir*) which offers itself to each agent as accessible inasmuch as it is the objective future (*l'avenir*) of the class to which he belongs. In Algeria, as in most developing countries, the most clear-cut division is that between the regular workers, manual or non-manual, and the mass of unemployed or intermittent workers, journeymen, labourers, or small traders, interchangeable statuses which often fall successively to the same individual. In fact, to each socio-economic position corresponds a system of practices and dispositions organized around the relationship to the future that is implied in that position. These systems of dispositions can be described synchronically as being distributed in accordance with the objective hierarchies of the socio-economic positions to which they correspond. But they can also be seen as stages in an ordinate process: if at moment t the disposition systems of two individuals of two social classes A and B are defined by socio-economic conditions X_A and X_B, then we may assume that at moment t_1 individual or class A, having acquired condition B, will adopt the behaviour which was that of B at moment t. We can then consider that a description of the disposition systems of the different social classes is at the same time a description of the different stages in the process of "rationalization".

In studying the process of workers' adaptation to the capitalist system and the assimilation of the categories which capitalism presupposes and demands, we

The disenchantment of the world

clearly cannot ignore the fact that the confrontation of societies, the clash of cultures, and the consequent economic and cultural changes take place under the pressure of the most implacable economic necessity and are only fully intelligible in relation to the colonial system, in other words the domination which forces the colonized to adopt the law of the colonizer as regards the economy and even their life-style, denying the dominated society the power of selection. So if one describes the process of adaptation to the economy imported by colonization as one of rationalization, it must not be forgotten that this economy is only *formally* rational and that, because it is based on an essential *contradiction*, it can gain in formal rationality only by losing in material rationality.

We can take it as established that the sheer pressure of economic necessity is sufficient to impose forced submission (the price of which is subsistence) to the economic order imported by colonization; that it can bring about the collapse of the norms and mental schemes which traditionally governed economic conduct; that it can also give rise to and sustain economic practices that are absurd both in terms of the spirit of the pre-capitalist economy and in terms of the logic of the capitalist economy. Does this mean to say that the economic necessity which can break a number of cultural resistances and make fidelity to the traditions untenable is in itself capable of producing a creative reinvention of new economic strategies and elective adherence to the ethos which, in the capitalist economic system, is linked to that capacity? If it is true that economic determinisms have to be eased before the possibility can arise of effectively subjecting economic practice to the imperatives of "rationalization", this means that rapid or gradual transformations of the economic habitus, which, we have seen, in some cases take place under the pressure of economic necessity, always remain dependent on material conditions. But must we therefore conclude that they are purely and simply imposed? In other words, if attaining a minimum of security is the necessary condition for the effective "rationalization" of conduct, is it also a sufficient condition for the effective formation of a system of goals the highest of which is the maximization of monetary income?

Condemned to instability, deprived of the patronage which the age-old traditions guaranteed to the meanest *khammes*, lacking the skills and qualifications which alone might win them the security they aspire to above all else, trapped in a hand-to-mouth existence and in chronic anxiety about the next day, the sub-proletarians – unemployed and casual journeymen, small traders, white-collar workers in small firms and shops, labourers – are kept absolutely incapable of calculating and forecasting by an economic system which demands forecasts, calculation, and the rationalization of economic conduct.

"Sometimes I work one day, sometimes four days, sometimes I'm out of work for a whole month. I have debts of almost 5,000 francs. I borrow on one side to repay on the other, that's the way it's always been. I've got no trade, no qualifications, how do you expect me to live? I work as a labourer, I carry water, I carry stones on building sites...If only I could get a job! You see I've been 'got by the throat'. When I'm not labouring, I go into town and I work as a porter in the market. I borrow left and right...I leave home at five in the morning and off I go. I look and look. Sometimes I come back at midday or one o'clock and I've still found nothing...! My earnings are like my work. Never regular, never certain. What can I do? I earn about 10,000 francs a month on average. I'd do anything to earn my family a living" (casual labourer, Constantine).

For these men, ready to do anything and conscious of being skilled at nothing, always available and totally subject to every determinism, without any true trade and therefore condemned to every sort of pseudo-trade, there is nothing solid, nothing certain, nothing permanent. The daily routine divided between searching for work and improvising work, the week or the month broken up into working days and idle days by chance hirings and lay-offs – everything is stamped with precariousness. No regular timetable, no fixed place of work; the same discontinuity in time and space. The search for work is the one constant factor in an existence swept to and fro by the whim of accident, together with the daily failure of that search. You look for work "left and right"; you borrow "left and right"; you borrow on the left to repay on the right. The whole of life is lived under the sign of the provisional. "My work", said a street trader in Tlemcen, "is just a makeshift, until something better turns up." Ill adapted to the urban world into which they have strayed, lacking a regular working life and the security given by the certain product of labour, deprived of the reassuring traditions of the village community, and forced to learn everything about both the urban world and the technical world – their language, their discipline, their skills – they strive with obstinate persistence to force the hand of chance and take hold of a present which escapes their grasp.

The disenchantment of the world

Unemployment leads to a systematic disorganization of conduct, attitude, and ideologies. By preventing him from fulfilling his economic function, it threatens the social function of the head of the family, in other words his authority within the family and his dignity outside it. The father, the brothers, the cousins, and sometimes even the wife and the children must supply the needs of the group. The extreme situation, that of men who are supported by their wives, is experienced both by the individual concerned and the group as the final degradation. "In my opinion", said an unemployed man in Oran, "a wife shouldn't work; it's forbidden. But we couldn't keep our heads above water, so she worked." And another, shaking his head to express the enormity of the situation: "Now it's my wife who works for me!" When it ceases to be seen as a temporary expedient, the permanence of such a state of dependence sometimes brings on a profound demoralization. Some street traders end up making an occupation of what was originally only a temporary makeshift. The same is true of some of the unemployed. Little by little a fatalistic resignation sets in; irresistibly, a parasitic existence becomes natural and then habitual. Being unemployed or doing non-jobs becomes a way of life, an occupation. The objective barriers, wild, impossible aspirations, pseudo-work and pseudo-efforts to find work, all provide excuses for giving up. More and more applications are made where there is a certainty of failure, a miracle is awaited, and "pick and shovel" work is increasingly shunned. Against exploitation and injustice the only weapons to hand are flight, cunning, and trickery, the *chtara* that is so often mentioned: anything will serve so long as it helps one to escape exploitation, to cut out a moment of hateful work and to earn one's wages with the least effort. These men, chained by need to a task which brings them nothing beyond the minimum they need to survive, have only one freedom left in their work: the freedom to express their subterranean revolt against exploitation by underproduction.

The lack of regular employment means not just the absence of a guaranteed wage but also the absence of the whole set of constraints which define a coherent organization of time and a system of coherent expectations. Like emotional equilibrium, the system of temporal and spatial frameworks within which existence unfolds cannot be constituted without the reference points supplied by regular work. The whole of life is abandoned to incoherence.[1] A man without work goes off in the morning, more or less early, depending on whether he really has hopes or is already resigned; all morning he walks from one building site to another, relying on the advice of a friend, a cousin, or a neighbour. He stops at a café and has a drink and a smoke with his friends. Looking for work becomes a whole occupation.

Unemployment or intermittent work sweep away the traditions

1. Perhaps there are grounds for seeing the absence of the precise spatio-temporal frameworks that are provided by regular work as one cause of uncertainty and even incoherence in opinions and judgements, particularly those regarding relatively abstract and general problems.

but prevent the working-out of a rational life-plan. "If you're not sure of today", said an unemployed man in Constantine, "how will you be sure of tomorrow?" And a fisherman in Oran: "The more I earn, the more I eat; the less I earn, the less I eat." These two formulae go to the heart of the existence of the sub-proletarians. The one goal of activity is the satisfaction of immediate needs. "I earn my hunk of bread, and that's all." "What I earn, I eat." "I earn just my children's bread." "I work to feed my children." Gone are the old traditions of foresight. The townsman tends to resemble the image which the traditional peasant had of him: "What the day has toiled at, the night has eaten." Sometimes one sees the reappearance of traditional practices, totally out of place in the new context, and inspired by the obsession with subsistence: "I have stocks of food set aside", said a small grocer in Oran earning 400 or 500 francs a day. "If ever I earn nothing, I'll eat all the same." This is the traditionalism of despair, as irrational as hand-to-mouth existence.

> Because the sacrifices bear mainly on consumption, income can increase without saving or even the idea of saving making its appearance, the needs are so much greater than the means. Furthermore, payment by the day, especially in the case of casual or regular day-labourers, prevents any rationalization. By parcelling out income into small sums immediately exchangeable for goods intended to be consumed the same day, it tends to rule out all expenditure on durable goods, which can only be conceived of (and paid off) over a long period.

Instead of the future (*l'avenir*) announcing itself in present conduct, instead of the present being organized in relation to a future (*un futur*) posited by calculation and connected rationally to the present, the present day is lived without any reference, whether rational or intuitive, to the next day. Primary needs are such that their satisfaction cannot be deferred or sacrificed. The sub-proletarians are totally barred from establishing a rational hierarchy of goals, the precondition for the calculation which is the basis of conduct defined as reasonable in terms of capitalist reason.

> An economic subject conforming to this description would rapidly meet with disaster if he found himself thrown into a perfectly rationalized economic and social universe. In reality, on the edges of the cities of Africa and South America there are economic universes which act as a sort of buffer between the sub-proletariat and the modern world. Their fundamental law seems to be the same as governs individual practices: the absence of predictability and calculability. The poorest and the most bewildered find there a number of safeguards which enable

them to achieve a precarious equilibrium, at the lowest level, in the absence of any calculation – mutual help among kinsmen and neighbours which furnishes assistance in money or kind during the search for work, or unemployment, sometimes the job itself; a place to live, a shared living space and kitchen which guarantee subsistence to the most desititute, with the pooling of wages and joint expenditure tending to compensate for the irregularity and smallness of each income; credit based on trust, etc.

Lacking that minimum hold on the present which is the precondition for a deliberate effort to take hold of the future (*le futur*), these men are unable to work out a life-plan, a coherent, hierarchized system of goals foreseen or projected, encompassing in the unity of a single outlook their present conduct and the future (*l'avenir*) which it works to bring about. Totally overwhelmed by a world which denies them any realizable future (*avenir*), they can only accede to a "future indefinite" (*un futur rêvé*) in which everything is possible, because there the economic and social laws which govern the universe of their daily existence are suspended. The unemployed man who, for himself, only aspires to a "good trade", to the permanent employment that an occupational skill would give him, can dream of "fine trades" for his son, "dream trades" as one of them put it, lawyer or doctor. These are two successive and mutually exclusive consciousnesses which aim at the present and at the future; the discourse often proceeds in a jagged line, the leaps into daydream being followed by relapses into a present that withers all fantasies. Short of a certain threshold of likelihood, only magical solutions remain. Magical hope is the outlook on the future characteristic of those who have no real future before them.

Insecurity and poverty are exacerbated by the disappearance of the whole set of guarantees which were formerly provided by the reassuring traditions of peasant society and which made possible customary foresight, dictated and sustained by common wisdom and based on temporal landmarks and frameworks which ensured a form of predictability.

Gone are the assurances provided by religion, which organized practices and representations in accordance with a single body of principles. Torn from the social environment in which they lived their whole lives and particularly their religious lives, deprived of the atmosphere of religiosity which emanated from collective life, placed in difficult conditions of existence and confronted with radically new problems, the proletariat and sub-proletariat of the towns can only choose between indifference and superstition – institutional piety, a series of gestures void of meaning, performed passively or mechanically and governed by unenthusiastic submission to a mutilated tradition. The break with tradition brought about by emigration, the relaxing of collective pressure linked to the anonymity of urban life, contact with a technical civilization entirely devoted to profane ends, the explicit and diffuse teachings of the school, all these influences combine to produce a thorough transmutation of values and to destroy the soil in which traditional religiosity was rooted.

Deprived of the material and psychological support given by the networks of relationships in peasant society and by the kinship groups that are now fragmented by emigration, too harassed to be able to take systematic cognizance of their condition and encompass in the sweep of an active intention the present that is undergone and the future that is desired, kept in a state of perpetual frustration and insecurity which leads them to hope for immediate satisfactions and expect the miracle that could rescue them from their condition, the sub-proletarians – landless peasants, farm workers, men without work, journeymen, casual labourers – will readily give ear to any eschatological prophecy which breaks with the routine of everyday existence and holds out, even if it means a radical transformation of society, the promise of again finding a place in the world, that is to say, both the material security and the sense of security given by a new social framework. Revolutionary chiliasm and magical utopias are the only grasp on the future that offers itself to a class without any objective future.

The workers are sharply divided into two groups, those who are stable and do all they can to remain so, and those who are unstable and are ready to do anything to escape from instability. This is the fundamental fact that has to be borne in mind in order to understand, among other things, the fascination exerted on the most underprivileged strata by stable occupations or, more precisely, the stability of occupations and, therefore, by vocational qualification and by education as the means of getting it. Jobs such as those of caretaker, night-watchman, orderly, or warden are also, in their own way, "dream jobs", not only because they are undemanding but also because they are the most reliable of those an individual without education, vocational training, or capital can get. The desire for stability, common to the great majority of unskilled workers, low-grade office workers, small tradesmen and craftsmen, takes the form of an aspiration to a genuine occupation – as opposed to just being busy – in which the conditions of hiring and lay-off, promotion and retirement are guaranteed and regulated, in which there is organized protection against cut-throat competition, and in which the regulations on health and safety, hours of work, standards of skill, and payment, are effectively implemented. If the civil service is syncretically perceived as an occupational paradise, that is because, even in the absence of union monitoring, it provides the minimum guarantees against arbitrariness and, above all, gives security, defined not so much by the amount of the wages as by their regularity.[2]

If it coincides with a readjustment of the system of aspirations, the achievement of regular employment does not necessarily bring about a reorganization of the goals of economic activity, which in most cases remains oriented towards the satisfaction of immediate needs. The ambition of the great majority of permanent workers is to be able to live "without having to count", in other words, without debts or savings. As soon as they can, they give up the use of credit based on confidence, which enabled the most underprivileged to secure a precarious balance between their aspirations and their resources. Economic conduct continues to obey the principle of maximizing security, and aspirations tend to be tailored more or less in relation to the available means. In a situation of structural unemployment, the very people who have achieved security continue to experience it as threatened and see themselves as privileged. When it makes its appearance, the desire to maximize income comes into conflict with the objective conditions of the labour market, which prevent a profitable increasing of effort. There is indignation that a bachelor can earn as much as a married

2. This explains much behaviour which might appear irrational if it were referred to the logic of the maximization of income. The following example is a case observed in Algiers in July 1960. A mechanic specializing in the maintenance of tractors and diesel engines was taken on as an employee by the Soil Defence and Restoration Department: he received a basic wage of 55,000 Old Francs, plus a danger allowance, travel expenses, and overtime, so that the average monthly income was 80,000 francs. On the advice of his father, he turned it down and got a job as a mechanic with the R.S.T.A. (Algerian Public Transport Authority), where his father was a conductor. He started at 36,000 francs a month, but he enjoyed all the advantages of public-sector employment – stability, pension, leave, etc. For the same reasons, craftsmen and tradesmen earning between 30,000 and 70,000 francs a month often envy the position of workers in the modern sector and, *a fortiori*, the public sector.

man, and disapproval of men who have more than one job and European women who work. There are many respondents who seem not to conceive that their labour power and labour time could be quantified, and who, in order to assess the wages they consider they deserve, take account of their needs and not of their effort or skill. However, opinions tend to become systematized: the gap between level of aspiration and level of achievement tends to close, both because hopes become more moderate and because the effective possibilities increase; by the same token, demands become more realistic.

The labour élite, relatively small in number owing to the limited development of industry, partake of the advantages supplied by the modern economy, family allowances, promotion, modern housing, schooling for their children, "privileges" which are inseparable from stability of employment and which are denied both to the sub-proletarians and to the semi-proletarians in the traditional sector. Do the attachment to these advantages and the contagion of needs by the effect of demonstration constitute obstacles to the formation of a revolutionary consciousness? In reality, only individuals equipped with a coherent system of aspirations and demands, capable of setting themselves within the logic of calculation and forecasting because their conditions of existence allow them to do so and because they have been able to acquire a progressive and rational attitude in their working life, can grasp their existence systematically and realistically by reference to a collective future and deliberately accept the sacrifices and renunciations that accompany any revolutionary action. And finally, being accustomed to submit to rational requirements and inclined to realism by the very nature of their daily activity, the proletarians are the group of workers least open to the seductions of demagogy.

Arrival at an income level between 60,000 and 80,000 francs a month coincides with a general transformation of conduct which is rooted in the emergence of a new relation to the future and is manifested in a whole set of objective indices, such as the multiplication of sources of income among those earning between 60,000 and 80,000 francs, the emergence of the hope of increasing financial gain without increasing effort, or what might appear to be the purely demographic fact that the average number of live births per married woman steadily increases with income until the income reaches 80,000 francs, declining sharply thereafter. Everything takes place as if arrival at an income level such that the preoccupation with subsistence disappears and basic needs are satisfied was the necessary condition for the individual to be able to wrench himself or herself from the crudest economic determinisms and strive towards a still absent goal beyond the present in which he or she was trapped by the pressure of needs demanding immediate satisfaction. The effort to master the future cannot be undertaken in reality until the conditions indispensable for ensuring it a minimum chance of success are actually provided. Until this is the case, the only possible attitude is forced traditionalism, which differs essentially from adherence to tradition, because it implies the possibility of acting differently and the impossibility of enacting that possibility.[3]

Though it clearly corresponds to a decisive transformation of the material conditions of existence, associated with a rising level of skill and education, this restructuring of the system of dispositions and ideologies is not the product of necessity alone, and presupposes an original systematization which each individual, making himself the entrepreneur of his own life, must carry out on his own behalf, because his behaviour in each area has to be the product of a thoroughgoing reinvention. The adoption and assimilation of the spirit of prediction and calculation vary in direct proportion to the degree of integration into an economic and social order defined by calculation and prediction. The most reliable and significant indices of this degree of integration are the degree of bilingualism and level of education.

> To explain why the degree of bilingualism increases with the degree of economic success, one can no doubt invoke the fact that the transformation of attitudes and the learning of French presuppose the same conditions, i.e. intense and prolonged contact with European society or the modern economy. However, everything takes place as if the use of Arabic were linked – *at a given moment in the history of the society and the language* – to the adoption of a whole world-view. Invocations of God or destiny, rare among French-speaking respondents, are very frequent among those expressing themselves in Arabic, whether enabling

3. This is seen very clearly among the peasants in intensively colonized regions, who will acknowledge the superior efficiency and profitability of the colonist's techniques, but continue to practise the traditional methods, because they know that the colonist's way of farming demands means which are not available to them and without which they would inevitably fail.

an embarrassing problem to be avoided or serving to conceal the absence of any definite opinion under diffuse well-meaning remarks. Respondents who express themselves in French generally show themselves to be more realistic and more revolutionary. Furthermore, those who have most difficulty with French often punctuate their remarks with sentences or phrases in garbled or correct French, mainly when expressing their poverty or their revolt. For those who are bilingual, switching from their mother tongue to French often has the same significance and the same function. The French language, especially as spoken in Algeria, is felt to be secularized, realistic, and "positive". For the Algerians it is, among other things, the language of real or imaginary dialogue with their bosses, and hence the language of bargaining for better pay and conditions.

In most cases, education and occupational skill provide the indispensable means enabling conduct based on foresight and calculation to be performed with a certain chance of success (stability and hopes of promotion, sufficient income, etc.), i.e. the necessary condition, while at the same time supplying the intellectual resources enabling conduct to be rationalized, i.e. the sufficient condition. Everything takes place as if the economic agent's existence had to be amenable to forecasting and calculation in order for him actually to be able to submit it to foresight and calculation. Only those with a future before them can undertake to master it.

If the restructuring of practices takes a systematic form, this is because, sharing a common reference to a calculated future, all forms of rational action – family planning, saving, concern for the children's education – are united by a structural affinity. For example, so long as people lack the minimum mastery of the present that would enable them to conceive the ambition of mastering the future, surrender to natural fertility imposes itself as the only means of gaining any sort of hold on the future; we may even suppose that the ideology handed down by tradition, whereby the child, and especially the boy, is a protection and an honour, takes on a new life in times of crisis, when the old securities are swept away, because to surround oneself with children is above all to surround oneself with protections. To delay child-bearing, on the other hand, is to sacrifice the present to the future, to refuse to let things simply take their course; it is to act in the present in relation to a calculated future. The restructuring of conduct only appears at a relatively high level of income (and not as soon as the security threshold is reached), because, precisely on account of the

The disenchantment of the world

systematic nature of the new life-style, restructuration has to be accomplished all at once, when all the economic and cultural conditions for the conversion of economic and cultural dispositions are united. Those individuals and families unable to bring together all the necessary conditions are condemned to encounter virtually insuperable contradictions when they endeavour to cross the line at a single point.

Thus, access to modern housing casts into a deep malaise individuals who do not have the means of satisfying all the needs linked to the satisfied need. This observation is all the more surprising, at first sight, because moving into a modern dwelling is marked, overall, by an undeniable improvement in living conditions:[4] the living-space index is 8, compared to 2.5 for the badly housed sample. The average number of rooms per family is 2.8 as against 1.5. Twenty per cent of the respondents have the same number of rooms as in their previous home, 27 per cent one room more, 33 per cent two more, and 18 per cent three more. The average available surface is 45 square metres as against 18.5 for the badly housed. Rehousing means the end of the single room or, at least, the big shared bedroom which is the lot of most shanty-town-dwellers: in 76.1 per cent of the cases, the parents and children

4. These analyses are mainly based on a survey in the summer of 1960 which took a representative sample of families (selected from the files of the building organizations) living in ten groups of modern dwellings – an estate in Philippeville, seven estates in Constantine (Les Mûriers, Le Bon Pasteur, Anatole France, El Bar, Les Apôtres, Les Platanes, Les Pins, and Cité Gaillard), and two estates in Algiers (Les Pins and La Concorde, Nobleterre). For comparative purposes use was also made of the results of analysis of a random sample of the housing requests received by the Service des H.L.M. (Municipal Housing Department) in Algiers, and observations and interviews in various shanty towns in Algiers and the Casbah in 1958 and 1959. Information from a survey in 1960 of a sample of families housed in modern dwellings, providing data on the whole domestic economy, was also used. The master sample in the survey of the newly housed accurately reflects the overall pattern of the tenants: labourers make up 17 per cent, semi-skilled or skilled workers 20.5 per cent, service staff 25.5 per cent, civil servants and armed forces 9 per cent, tradesmen and craftsmen 15.5 per cent, senior executives 2.5 per cent, and retired or non-employed 10 per cent. Ninety-seven per cent of the respondents are of urban origin, and, generally having regular employment and incomes, are particularly well placed to adapt to the demands of their new accommodation (so that all the analyses which follow are valid *a fortiori* for those not exhibiting these characteristics). Thirty-six per cent of the respondents have been in their new dwelling less than a year, 65 per cent less than two years. (The main findings of this survey have been assembled in a synoptic table, because they do not appear in *Travail et travailleurs en Algérie*.)

Synoptic table of monthly housing expenditure variations by social class

Socio-occupational category	Size of family (average)	No. economically active	Monthly income (average) (Old Francs)	Average rent	(%)	Average service charges	(%)	Average rent and services	(%)	Average transport	(%)	Average upkeep	(%)	Average furniture	(%)	Average total expenditure	(%)
Labourers	5.6	1.13	41,818	9,091	(21.5)	5,000	(12.0)	14,091	(33.5)	750	(1.5)	1,022	(2.5)	3,522	(8.5)	19,385	(46.5)
Operatives	6.4	1.18	52,307	9,166	(17.5)	5,100	(9.5)	14,266	(27.0)	2,721	(5.0)	3,173	(6.0)	4,388	(8.5)	24,548	(46.5)
Service staff	6.5	1.24	65,000	9,758	(15.0)	5,338	(8.0)	15,096	(23.0)	2,780	(4.0)	5,348	(8.0)	8,181	(12.5)	31,405	(48.0)
Craftsmen and tradesmen	6.6	1.35	57,000	7,236	(12.5)	4,000	(8.0)	11,836	(21.0)	2,075	(3.5)	4,578	(8.0)	7,550	(13.0)	26,039	(45.5)
Public sector: civil and military	6.6	1.33	106,250	12,500	(11.5)	7,000	(6.5)	19,500	(18.0)	2,666	(2.5)	6,208	(6.0)	3,000	(3.0)	31,474	(29.5)
Retired	5.5	0.54	54,615	9,318	(17.0)	4,423	(8.0)	13,841	(25.0)	3,583	(7.5)	2,076	(4.0)	10,846	(20.0)	30,346	(56.0)
All	6.3	1.16	60,664	9,274	(15.5)	5,209	(8.5)	14,483	(24.0)	2,293	(3.5)	3,754	(6.0)	6,646	(11.0)	27,176	(44.5)

The disenchantment of the world

sleep in separate rooms (only 14.6 per cent of the families still share the same bedroom). So one might expect to record only statements of satisfaction; but in fact only 47 per cent of the respondents say they are satisfied, while 38 per cent express various degrees of discontent (the others remaining undecided).

Because rehousing generally leads to the splitting-up of large families which the housing crisis forced to live together, with the family group tending to be reduced to the couple, the number of employed persons per family declines.[5] In the old home, economic equilibrium was usually based on a plurality of sources of income, as against joint expenditure, on both housing and food. This balance is therefore endangered at the moment when all types of expenditure, particularly those related to housing, increase sharply. The average number of persons in each family is 6.3: this still very high figure is much lower than that found in the survey of the badly housed, 8.6. The difference looks even greater when it is borne in mind that the number of children is, officially, one of the criteria determining who should be rehoused.[6] The fall in the average number of persons is due to the fact that one section of the "extended family" which had been reconstituted under the pressure of necessity has remained in the old dwelling while the other section has come to live in the H.L.M. (municipal housing). This is confirmed by the fact that the proportion of nuclear families is much greater in the rehoused sample than in the sample living in precarious conditions.[7]

Seventy-seven per cent of the families contain one economically

5. An indication that urban life and the life-style it imposes favour the progressive disintegration of the extended family may be seen in the fact that average family size is inversely related to the size of the city: 7.2 in Philippeville, 6.9 in Constantine, and 5.2 in Algiers. This is accounted for in part by a parallel decline in the average number of children (Philippeville 4.06, Constantine 3.08, Algiers 2.95); but the fact remains that the ideal of the extended family is most distorted and most burdensome where adaptation to urban life is most developed.
6. Priority in rehousing was given to those who were badly housed but earning a relatively regular and high income. We have seen that in Algeria the number of children tends to rise with income (up to a certain threshold).
7. On the other hand, although the average number of children has fallen slightly (3.29 per family instead of 3.83) because of the separation of couples previously living in the same household, rehousing and the accompanying improvement in hygiene and comfort have led to a decline in the infant mortality rate (as is shown by comparing the number of children who, according to the fertility tables, ought to have been born after rehousing with the actual number of births). This short-term increase in fertility coincides, in the most privileged families, with the appearance of a tendency towards increased birth control, one dimension of a total disposition which finds the conditions for its realization in the new dwelling and the new life-style now possible.

active person and 14.5 per cent two, and the average for the whole sample is 1.16; this compares with 1.67 for the badly housed families, 20 per cent of which contain three or more active persons (as against only 3 per cent here). This tends to confirm that the reduction of the domestic group mainly results from the family having shed a certain number of adults who previously lived with it (generally the father, mother, or brothers of husband or wife). This phenomenon has important consequences: in the old dwelling, a very low rent was met by several adults of working age, whereas now the considerably higher housing costs tend to be supported by a single wage packet. The whole of the old equilibrium, based on plurality of incomes and joint expenditure, is jeopardized at the very moment when expenses of all sorts are increased.

In the badly housed sample (inhabitants of the Algiers Casbah or the shanty towns), the average number of economically active persons per family was relatively high, especially in those categories where the wages of the head of the family are lowest, so that they can only live by combining several small wages (retired people, labourers, tradesmen and craftsmen, and, to a lesser extent, service staff). By forcing several heads of families to share the same dwelling and necessitating the survival of the old solidarities, which urban life and the logic of the money economy had undermined, the housing shortage has the paradoxical effect of enabling an unexpected type of adaptation to take place: the real unit is not the couple (*le ménage*) but the "household" (*la maisonnée*); and a grouping of individuals or couples pooling a number of small wages lives incomparably less badly than each couple would on a single wage. Group solidarity provides each individual or couple with guarantees against material and psychological destitution: the irregularity of their earnings is offset by family mutual aid and confidence-based credit which ensure a minimum of regularity in consumption despite the uncertainty of incomes and the absence of rational calculation. Thus, with the aid of pooled wages and family allowances, 48 per cent of the families receive an income of more than 70,000 francs a month, and 72 per cent of them more than 50,000 francs. Their expenses are relatively low (especially when compared to what they will be in their new homes): the rent is generally fairly small; the shopkeepers in the old quarters of the city and the shanty towns sell second-quality goods but at very low prices; they also give credit; travel expenses are relatively low because it has been possible to choose the dwelling for the sake of its proximity to the place of work. Thus, on similar wages, people live better in a shanty town than in an H.L.M. The shanty town partakes of an economic universe which has a logic of its own and which enables the least well equipped to achieve a form of adaptation to the urban world. Although, superficially, it presents all the appearances of the contrary, the economy of poverty has its coherence. The shanty town even has its labour market, which is able to provide at least a semblance of work (with the minor improvised occupations), and its network of information as to the chances of employment.

This old equilibrium, which required several couples to live together, since, with only very rare exceptions, only the *men* work, cannot be replaced by a new equilibrium based in part on the women's work, as is the case in European households, which, in the same estates, have an average income that is twice as high (122,900 francs a month as against 60,600), because they earn higher average wages and also because 15 per cent of the wives work in relatively well-paid occupations (compared to 4.5 per cent of the Algerian women). A number of obstacles, not all of which, at least in the most privileged strata, are cultural, such as the women's lack of education, prevent this substitution (at least temporarily). And the fact that, for lack of education, Algerian women generally only have access to jobs considered to be degrading (such as that of charwoman), provides reinforcement or justification for the men's resistance to the women's working. Thus rehousing leaves many couples stranded between a lost equilibrium, the one which ensured the forced survival of the old extended family, with several wages as against joint expenditure, and a new equilibrium that is forbidden or unobtainable. The average family income (60,600 francs) is markedly lower than that of the badly housed (74,000 francs), although the average wage is markedly higher (which mitigates the fall in income caused by the reduced number of economically active persons).

The average number of persons per family having fallen at the same time as income, the average income per person is higher than before for the rehoused sample (9,629 francs as against 8,604 francs). But it is doubtful whether this (relatively large) difference is sufficient to offset the new expenditure incurred on moving into a modern dwelling. For the average monthly rent rises from around 3,000 francs for the badly housed to 9,200 francs in the new accommodation. The fact that the badly housed said they were prepared to pay 10,500 francs a month, which is more than they actually pay for their new dwelling, does not prevent us from understanding why the rehoused complain in particular about the dearness of their rent. It is only an apparent contradiction and stems from a phenomenon of dual contextualization which needs to be analysed.

Seventy-six per cent of the badly housed pay a rent of less than 3,000 francs (and only 4 per cent of the total have rents of more than 10,000 francs); 73 per cent of them spend less than 5 per cent of their family income on rent. The high rate of "don't knows" means that care must be taken in the use of information concerning the maximum rent they say they would be prepared to pay; but it may be noted that 52 per cent of them were willing to pay a rent of more than 10,000 francs, and that the average of the maximum acceptable rents (10,241 francs) was 3.5 times higher than their real rents. Such a discrepancy is not explained simply by the fact that the desire to escape from precarious or critical conditions of existence is so great as to rule out purely economic calculation. No doubt it is true that catastrophic living conditions lead people to confer inordinate importance on getting new housing (as is evidenced by, *inter alia*, the large number of requests and applications which the respondents had made). But this overestimation of the sacrifice to be made is encouraged, above all, by the fact that incomparable things are being compared – a certain budgetary equilibrium achieved in the Casbah or shanty town, and new conditions whose economic consequences are ill assessed in advance. When the badly housed accept the possibility of a very high rent (10,421 francs on average), they are implicitly making reference to their present economic situation. But the economic equilibrium they achieve in their precarious environment presupposes a certain number of conditions which will not necessarily be fulfilled in the new environment: several incomes, a low cost of living, virtually no service charges, etc.

The proportion of their income that the rehoused spend on their rent is 15.3 per cent on average, compared to 4.7 per cent among the badly housed (who declared themselves willing to spend on rent 13 per cent of a considerably higher family income). This enormous difference is due to the combined effect of the fall in average family income and the increased amount of the rents. Like all expenses per person, rent has increased by a higher proportion than average income per person: whereas, in the badly housed sample, it was 3,000 francs for an average family of 8.6 persons, it is now 9,200 francs for a family unit of 6.3 persons (so that the average rent per person has *trebled*, rising from 348 francs to 1,472 francs).

As well as weighing heavily on the family budget, rent brings with it the notion of *fixed, regular payment dates*. Whereas, in the

The disenchantment of the world

shanty town or the Casbah, all sorts of arrangements were possible, since it was always possible to ask the landlord for an extension or borrow the small sum necessary to pay the instalment from a relative or friend, this is no longer the case in a housing estate or an H.L.M. The flexibility of personal relationships gives way to bureaucratic rigidity. Because it absorbs a major proportion of family income, and because it has to be paid at regular intervals and on specified dates, the rent (to which are added various service charges) becomes the centre of the whole pattern of budgeting and the whole domestic economy. It entails the necessity of disciplining and rationalizing expenditure. By virtue of the size and regularity of the commitment which it represents, it forbids – by the threat of serious disequilibrium – irregularity and instability in jobs and incomes, incoherence in purchasing, in short everything which characterized the economic life of the great majority of the badly housed people in the Casbah and the shanty towns and which still pervades the existence of the least-well-off among the new inhabitants of the estates.

The increase in the old expenses, such as rent, is aggravated by the appearance of new expenses such as transport costs and service charges. The new urban housing developments are mostly on the edges of the towns, so that many workers find themselves much further from their place of work as a result of rehousing. Moreover, many estates are totally without facilities like schools and shops and the children often have to go to school by public transport. In some cases long journeys are necessary in order to carry out administrative procedures, or to bring in supplies from the city centre or neighbourhoods where things are cheaper (it is not uncommon, for example, for people to continue to go and do their shopping in the area where they used to live).[8]

> Average monthly spending on travel is 2,300 francs (compared to 3,000 for the Europeans). But there are considerable variations between the different social categories: civil servants and service employees spend 2,600 francs and 2,700 francs per month, labourers 750 francs. So it seems that individuals in the least-well-off categories make savings on this item. It is among these groups, and particularly the labourers, that one finds the highest proportion who walk to work.

8. Thirty-two of those who say they would like to move house give as a reason their desire to live closer to where they work (the average journey time between home and work is twenty minutes; 20 per cent of the heads of families have a journey of more than half an hour).

Service charges amount on average to 5,000 francs a month (8.5 per cent of income). It is known that, of the badly housed, 64 per cent had running water, 64 per cent electricity, and only 20 per cent gas, and also that the low-wage categories (labourers, operatives, service employees) were those most lacking in means of comfort. So it is the economically least-favoured categories, those for whom the rent burden is proportionately greatest, that experience the sharpest increase in service charges. Although the contrast is lessened by the efforts made by the families with the lowest incomes to curb this expenditure, the sum devoted to service charges does not vary in the same way as income, and it is in the lowest-income categories that the proportion taken by this item in total spending is greatest. One can imagine the unease felt by low-income families faced with the dilemma of whether to make unstinting use of the facilities offered by their new accommodation, at the price of completely unbalancing the family budget or making sacrifices in other areas, food for example, or to reduce as far as possible the proportion of income devoted to service charges by refraining from using the water-heater, and reducing their consumption of gas, water, and electricity. But how can the total conversion that is indispensable to ensure a rational management of the budget, an even distribution of wages over time, and a balanced allocation of expenditure between the various items, be expected of families (and particularly of women) who, only ever having known village traditions and shanty-town poverty, do not have the material and cultural means of bringing their everyday existence under the control of rationality, calculation, and rational forecasting? But this is not all: to opt to restrict as far as possible the spending caused by the use of household facilities would mean deliberately denying yourself everything you had previously been denied. That would amount to putting yourself back in a shanty-town life-style but in totally new conditions: there is an abyss between not having gas when you live in a shanty town and being obliged to turn it off, when it is there, inside your own flat, and to go back to the *kanun* (terracotta brazier), so as to save money. The very fact of having moved into new housing becomes retrospectively absurd. In either case, modern housing paradoxically becomes the obstacle to the entry into modern life which it seemed to promise.

The same is true of furniture. In this area too, the heaviest expenses bear on the least-well-off. The better-off among the rehoused are likely to have owned some furniture already (when their living conditions allowed). The others mostly had only the bare minimum of equipment, since a prime effect of a precarious environment is that it rules out expenditure on furniture and household equipment in general. There are several convergent reasons for this. First, there is a lack of space and the "furniture" has to be reduced to the strict minimum: mattresses that are spread out at night and heaped in a corner by day, sometimes an improvised bed, made from planks resting on trestles, a wardrobe or sideboard for clothes and the most valuable objects. Secondly, even if the occupants had enough room, they would not think of really furnishing such a rudimentary dwelling, in which the furniture would quickly deteriorate. For these reasons, spending on decorating and furnishing is kept to the strict minimum (whereas spending on secondary items, such as a radio and occasionally a television set, and especially a scooter or car, is sometimes disproportionately great). In modern housing, on the other hand, the absence of furniture, which was one of the conditions of the rational use of living space, appears as a sort of scandalous absurdity; it objectively testifies to the occupants' incapacity to take real possession of the space available, an inability to adopt the modern life-style which such housing offers.[9]

Thus, the average percentage of expenditure more or less directly related to the home (rent, service charges, transport, upkeep, and furniture) is 44.5 per cent, as against less than 10 per cent amongst the badly housed (only 4.5 per cent of whose income went on rent with very low service charges, upkeep, and furniture expenditure). The whole economic life of the rehoused family has to be restructured around this item, which takes on an inordinate importance. The labourers, who have the lowest incomes (41,918

9. The sort of possession that is at issue here has nothing to do with ownership. Although the great majority (82 per cent) of them were tenants, the inhabitants of the shanty towns and the Casbah had less difficulty in taking possession of their homes than the estate-dwellers, of whom 9 per cent are owner-occupiers, 55 per cent virtual owners (buying their flats by instalments), and only 36 per cent tenants. The feeling of being unable to take real possession of the flat eventually takes away all meaning from the sense of ownership; so much so that a number of people buying their own flats by instalments [*location-vente*] say they would like to be flat-owners, when they virtually are so already.

francs a month), devote 21.5 per cent of their income to rent (compared to 15.5 per cent of the whole sample and 8 per cent for the senior executives); although they minimize their electricity and especially their gas consumption (either by using only the *kanun* or by turning off the water-heater), they still have to pay 5,000 francs, 12 per cent of their income, in service charges. In other words, these two items absorb exactly a *third* of their resources. Although their spending on the upkeep of their flats and on furniture is doubtless kept as low as possible (taking together only 11 per cent of income as against 17 per cent for the whole sample), housing-related expenditure takes up almost half their income.[10] This is a severe imbalance, and it is only by cutting back on other items, such as food and clothing, that these families can keep going in accommodation which causes them expenditure disproportionate to their means. Among the operatives, whose average wages are considerably higher, the share of expenditure devoted to the home remains much the same (45.6 per cent): rent and service charges take up similar sums (14,266 francs as against 14,091 for the labourers), but their transport costs (2,721 francs compared to 750 francs, 3.6 times as much), their upkeep costs (3,173 compared to 750 francs, 4.2 times as much), and their spending on furniture (4,388 compared to 3,522, 1.2 times as much) are much greater (by more than 5,000 francs). Perhaps it should be concluded that, of the restrictions people impose on themselves, the most disagreeable (those they abandon as soon as they are able) are, first, those concerning the upkeep and facilities of their homes, next, transport costs, and then furniture. In this category too, expenditure related to housing takes up almost half the incomes.[11] For the other categories, the situation is very different: first of all, there is a much smaller gap between expen-

10. If the proportion spent on furniture is relatively high (8.4 per cent compared to 10.9 per cent for the whole sample), this is because most of these families were totally without furniture when they were rehoused.
11. Craftsmen and tradesmen are, of all the categories, the one which devotes the lowest proportion of its income to rent and service charges (12.5 per cent and 8 per cent); but there is a very marked contrast between traditional craftsmen and tradesmen who have retained a traditional life-style, and hence very limited requirements as regards housing, and modern craftsmen who spend relatively large sums on the interior of their homes. Service staff, whose occupational activity brings them into contact with Europeans, and sometimes takes them into their homes, have (relatively) higher expenditure on upkeep and furniture – 13,529 francs a month, which is more than the labourers and the operatives together (4,544 francs and 7,561 francs respectively).

diture in the old home and in the new one. The middle and upper classes were already supplied with comforts and often paid a relatively high rent; because their incomes are greater, rent and service charges weigh less heavily on their budgets; and their families are much better prepared to adapt to a modern dwelling and to accept the disciplines demanded by that adaptation. Their sacrifices are offset by the advantages which a relatively high income renders accessible. So, as income rises, and with it educational level and degree of adaptation to modern life, modern housing ceases to be the sort of "poisoned gift" which it is for the lower categories and provides the material conditions for a reorganization of the system of practices.

The modern apartment is an element in a system and, as such, it requires its occupants to adopt a certain life-style; it presupposes and calls for the adoption of a whole complex of practices and representations, such as new relationships between members of the family, a new conception of the children's education, in a word, a new domestic economy. Accession to this environment demands a cultural metamorphosis which not all the rehoused are capable of because they have neither the economic means of achieving it, nor the dispositions – which cannot be formed in the absence of those means.

The modern apartment is an already structured space indicating by its organization, its extent, and its form the future use which can be made of it, the type of occupation it calls for, etc. As a tool, that is, a material object prepared for a certain use, it announces its future and the future use that one can (and must) make of it if one wants to conform to the "intention" it contains. In short, it appears as a system of demands inscribed in objective space and asking to be fulfilled, a universe strewn with expectations and thereby generating needs and dispositions. But at the same time, insofar as it is not perfectly and totally completed, insofar as additions and modifications are possible and even indispensable, the future use which can be made of it is never entirely predetermined. This is why it presents itself both as the site of demands to be satisfied and as an alien space to be cleared, humanized, in other words, possessed – and a space which resists. Transforming an apartment, furnishing it, decorating it, means, no doubt, making it more comfortable, but also and especially it means mastering it by imprinting one's mark on it, possessing it by making it personal. "Modern", made for a "modern" man, the apartment demands the behaviour of a modern man. For those who lack the means to occupy it and inhabit it, it becomes a sort of alien world on which they cannot imprint their mark and whose expectations they do not know how to fulfil. The arrangement of the rooms, the available space, the functional predeterminations call for a certain type of furniture, certain lighting, certain decoration. Nothing is more desolate than a modern apartment "furnished", as in a shanty town, with a few mattresses, a *kanun*, and a straw mat. This is because it is not lived in but "occupied": not a dwelling, an organized, mastered, humanized space, but merely "premises". The scandal is all the greater for the occupants themselves because they confusedly hoped that the modern apartment could satisfy expectations which it in fact arouses without helping to fulfil; greater too because, contrary to what happened in the shanty town, incitements and solicitations are no longer found (intermittently) in an alien universe, that of the Europeans, but are permanently inscribed in the most familiar space.[12]

In short, a modern apartment gives rise to sometimes insuperable material difficulties as well as inaccessible aspirations. Furthermore, by its very structure, it is linked to a whole art of living which the daily existence of many new tenants contradicts in every respect. By a sort of displacement, the person who finds himself incapable of fulfilling the requirements of his apartment comes to think that the accommodation does not satisfy his own requirements. Deciphering the intention contained in accommodation that is defined as "economical" or "intermediate" (*évolutif*), he perceives it as an inferior version of European housing, housing "built for Arabs and fit for Arabs" – when the accommodation he finds inadequate, because it is second-rate, in fact already exceeds his possibilities. Hence the contradictory statements of unhappy ten-

12. One of the foundations of the real solidarity between all the inhabitants of the shanty town is the uniformity of their conditions of existence, which causes poverty to be experienced as a common condition, shared by the whole group. The revolt of the excluded, which springs from comparison with the world, both different and external, of the Europeans, is quite different in nature from that aroused by direct experience of the impossibility of enjoying the advantages offered by that world, which are now within reach, in one's own home, in the form of a comfort which one has to deny oneself, or in the flat or building next door, in the homes of those who have the means of enjoying it.

ants who declare that they could afford the rent to live on the European estate (with "all mod. cons.") when in reality they have difficulty in meeting the rent and gas bills in their "economical" housing. Hence too the constellation of practices by which those who cannot adapt to the estate adapt the estate to themselves. Unable to achieve the higher level of adaptation required by the modern estate, they seek to create a form of adaptation at a lower level, at the cost of a "shanty townization" of the estate.[13] Thus, in the poorest classes, the extended family, which had split up, tends to be reconstituted. Relatives who had remained in the shanty town or have recently arrived from the country come and join the nucleus that is established in the apartment. On single-storey estates (La Montagne, for instance), shacks are built in the courtyards. Where there are tall blocks, the loggias are closed off and turned into rooms to house extra couples. The number of economically active persons increases. The new arrivals seek to make work for themselves on the perimeter of the estate, setting up small mobile businesses or spreading out their wretched, miscellaneous wares on the ground. At the same time, some of the European-style shops are abandoned. Meeting-places spring up spontaneously around the estate. Groups of old men are again to be seen leaning against the walls of the building, talking all day, as they did in the shanty town or in their village in Kabylia. But those who turn a modern estate into a shanty town are not obeying a backward-looking traditionalism. Prevented from adapting, as they wished, to an environment which requires a transformation of all their attitudes, deprived of the material conditions for such a transformation, they are simply re-creating the previous living conditions which they thought they were leaving behind them when they arrived in a modern estate.

The contrast between the needs aroused by the housing and the

13. The amount of vandalism in the shared parts of the estates, committed by the children and adolescents but rarely arousing strong disapproval in the parents, is perhaps the best indication of the lack of commitment to and, so to speak, refusal of responsibility for, the environment. On one estate (Diar-Mahçoul), where there is strong discontent, perhaps because it contains in an extreme form all the contradictions which have been analysed (the "intermediate" estate is next to the "all mod. cons." European estate; a number of tenants have relatively low incomes and so have great difficulty in adapting to their accommodation; and all sorts of obstacles stand in the way of the "shanty townization" that is possible in other "intermediate" estates, such as La Montagne), there is a very high degree of vandalism. Other estates (like Diar el Bahia), occupied by families who earn high wages and are co-owners of their buildings, have been very little vandalized.

means available is aggravated by the disturbance which results from moving into the new apartment and which touches every aspect of existence. Not only is the balanced budget which depended on there being several sources of income jeopardized by the fact that there generally remains only one wage, and sometimes an irregular one, to meet increased expenditure that has to be organized around what have become regular commitments,[14] but also the splitting up of the family and the break with a familiar neighbourhood lead to the isolation of the nuclear family and a slackening of the bonds of solidarity. There is no one to go for a stroll with; the lively atmosphere of the shanty town has given way to the superficial, occasional relationships of the housing estate; some go back to the shanty town in their spare time, to see their old friends, or go and sit in the shanty town adjacent to their building. The women in particular suffer from this contraction of the social field (surrounded by strangers, they go out less), all the more so since there is nothing in the home to take the place of their old relationships.[15]

The new environment isolates people whereas the shanty town or old neighbourhood united them. In a house in the Casbah, for instance, the separation between the dwellings occupied by different couples is more symbolic than real. The house or neighbourhood is the extension of the internal space of the home.[16] The wife's living space extends as far the neighbouring houses or rooms, and also as far as the fountain and grocery store; the flat or shack is surrounded by a whole set of variously distant points corresponding to different aspects of female activity, tasks which bring together increasingly large groups as the distance grows. In the corner of the room set aside for that purpose, the woman cooks; in the courtyard she gets water and sometimes does her

14. In contrast to confidence-based credit, bank credit imposes a hitherto unknown regularity and rigidity. The new expenses become the focus of all conduct. Stable expenditure entails stable employment and a certain amount of rational calculation.
15. Some men, aware of this privation, buy a television set for their wives. But such a purchase is out of the question for the poorest, who are hard put to it to pay their rent.
16. "In the Casbah, I knew everybody and everybody knew me. I could go into all the houses and visit the women. I could complain to people without there being trouble. Relationships with other people were no problem. There was only a veil between us. Here it isn't a veil, it's a door. There are 245 tenants here and we don't even know one another. We hardly say hello. Everyone goes home and shuts the door and that's all you see of them."

washing; on the terrace, she hangs out her washing; at the Turkish bath, shared by the whole district, she meets her neighbours. Thus most of the activities which fall to her help to insert her into a social network outside the family proper.

By contrast, the domestic cell in a residential block has to provide its occupants with everything they need. All the women's activities (washing, drying, ironing, cooking, etc.) can be carried out within it. This means that the opposition between the inside and the outside now corresponds exactly to the opposition between the family nucleus and the neighbourhood, between the apartment and the rest of the building. Because of the complete absence of collective facilities on the estate, the scope of the wife's activity is narrowed, especially since a modern flat offers more housework to be done; the outside world begins at the front door. Even the elevated passageway, which might be expected to create a link between neighbours, is foreign territory: it is rare, for example, for people to use it to take the evening air, or to leave pot plants on it. Since contacts with neighbours now only take place when housework is being done, they become rarer and more superficial, and when they do occur, they are seen as useless, as a waste of time in gossip or chatter. Moreover, perceived as an obstacle to the individualism which this environment encourages, social life is something one puts up with rather than chooses. Contacts very often only occur in the quarrels provoked by noise or the children. The change of residence means that people are no longer linked to their neighbours by the old ties, and the objective organization of space does not favour the establishment of new relationships. This results in an apparently contradictory attitude towards the new co-residents: people complain both of isolation (especially the women) and of overcrowding, mere proximity that is suffered, not sought. Because their cultural traditions have not prepared them for the new life-style and the smallness of the apartment encourages them to go out as soon as they can, the men continue to spend their leisure time together. Because their living space is greater and their natural place is outside, they suffer less than the women from the isolation due to rehousing. There is nothing to compensate the women for the loss of the satisfactions given by the social environment of the shanty town. Thus the nuclear family, with modern housing favouring its material and affective autonomization by the spatial and budgetary constraints it imposes, cannot find within itself either the economic resources or the cultural traditions (leisure activities, reading, home improvement, cultural images favouring and valorizing the privacy of the couple) which are the precondition for a full achievement of that autonomy. It follows that the new social units arising from rehousing find themselves halfway between two forms of economic and social equilibrium, with the sense of having lost everything on one side without gaining much on the other.

Conversely, for the most privileged categories, whose old environment condemned them to a dual existence, with a clear separation between the life they led at the office and the life the shanty town forced on them, access to modern housing is the opportunity for a cultural transformation. All obstacles are removed. The focus of all their contradictions disappears. Their living space now matches their possibilities. Their aspirations are redoubled by the incitements created by their home environment; or rather, desires which hitherto were formulated only in imagination and were concretely thwarted now find the material conditions for their realization. The tendency towards the self-completion of the system constituted by the new life-style gives rise to new needs. Certain forms of expenditure are greatly increased: furniture, labour-saving devices, clothes (with the desire to affirm a certain status), means of entertainment (television), etc. It follows that the breakdown of expenditure between the various items in the family budget is profoundly altered; more and more use is made of bank credit, which brings with it the need for calculation. It seems that spending on food is often reduced, at least in relative terms. However, unlike the other categories, who spend on housing amounts that are disproportionate to their incomes but without managing to satisfy the demands of a modern apartment and the new needs it stimulates, families in these classes are generally better prepared for adapting to a modern dwelling and undertaking the disciplines needed in order to succeed in such an adaptation; furthermore, with their considerably higher incomes, they are able to achieve a new economic equilibrium without having to make inordinate sacrifices in other areas. Because all the economic and cultural conditions for an overall transformation of the system of economic dispositions are united, access to modern housing is the opportunity for a restructuring of the system of practices which is to be seen in the division of labour between the sexes, the management of the family budget, the education of the children, and leisure activities. Thus the self-enclosure of the family group that is favoured by the new home environment is generally accompanied by the discovery of a new art of living: what for others is isolation is here experienced as privacy. The men spend much more time at home; reading, television, and the children increasingly take the place of time spent with friends. The women devote more time to housework, reading, and looking after the children who go to school. Intensified domestic relationships compensate for the increased rarity of outside relationships and the slackening of relationships with variously distant kinsmen which is both the precondition and the product of embourgeoisement.[17]

Thus, through the conditions which give access to it and the transformations of practice which it makes possible, modern housing has made possible the development of a (petty) bourgeoisie whose whole life-style, its values and its aspirations, separates it from the proletariat and sub-proletariat of the shanty towns and old urban areas. The conditions required of those who cross the "threshold of modernity" are such that it is here a boundary between classes.

17. Whereas the sub-proletarians, ill-adapted to the estate, maintain their links with their old circles, most members of this new middle class break their old connections, carefully avoiding any return to their old neighbourhood, and increasingly often abandoning the ritual of exchanged visits which previously maintained their ties with relatives remote in geographical and especially social space.

Conclusion

If the same meaning can express itself as much in economic conduct, whether fatalistic or enterprising, incoherent or methodical, as in political conduct and opinions, whether resigned or resolved, revolted or revolutionary, this is because the system of dispositions is linked to the economic and social situation through the mediation of the objective potentialities defined by and defining that situation. Objective, collective probabilities (such as the likelihood of access to scarce assets or the chances of upward mobility over one or several generations) – statistically measurable in the form of regularities independent of individual wills – are also concrete data in individual experience. Class habitus, the internalization of the objective situation, is the structure unifying the system of dispositions, which presuppose practical reference to the objective future, whether it be a matter of resignation to or revolt against the present order or the capacity to subject economic conduct to forecasting and calculation.

In fact, consciousness of class situation can also be, in another respect, an unconsciousness of that situation. The use of mediating (or hybrid) concepts, such as objective potentiality or class habitus, enables us to get beyond the abstract oppositions between the subjective and the objective, the conscious and the unconscious. The objective future is that which the observer has to postulate in order to understand the present behaviour of social subjects, which does not mean that he places in the consciousness of the subjects whom he observes the consciousness he has of their consciousness. For the objective future may not be a goal consciously pursued by the subjects and yet can still be the objective principle of all their conduct – because it is inscribed in those subjects' present situation and in their habitus, internalized objectivity, a permanent disposition acquired in a situation, under the influence of that situation. Both in their conscious representations and in their practices, the sub-proletarians reproduce the situation of which they are the product and which contains the impossibility of an adequate cognizance of the truth of the situation: they do not know that truth, but they enact it, or, if you will, they state it only in their actions. Their unrealistic statements only seem to contradict the objective reality which their acts so clearly express: illusion itself is not illusory and it would be a mistake to see an arbitrary phantasm in what is only the objective effect of their impossible position in the economic and social system.

Although the social agent necessarily cannot grasp as a totality a system which only ever appears to him in profiles, the gap between subjective apprehension and the objective truth of the situation varies considerably from one class situation to another. The pressure of economic necessity can arouse a discontent and a revolt which do not necessarily presuppose a clear, rational grasp of the goal of the revolt (as is seen for example in the distance between emotional quasi-systematization and genuine totalization) and which may manifest themselves in resigned passivity as well as in elementary explosions devoid of explicit purpose.[1] The mechanical image of compression and explosion too often obscures the fact that the most intense oppression does not coincide with the most acute awareness of oppression but that, on the contrary, it is precisely here that the discrepancy between the objective situation and awareness of that situation is greatest. In short, if we refuse to see class consciousness either as the mechanical result of the pressure of economic necessity or as the reflexive act of a freedom deciding itself despite and against all

1. It would seem that these analyses are as valid for the inhabitants of *favelas, barriadas,* and *brazzavilles* as for the inhabitants of the Algerian shanty towns, as is shown by two descriptions very close to those presented here. The first relates to Latin America and the second to Africa. "To me, among the striking things about these families are their general *malaise*, the rarity among them of happiness or contentment...It is characteristic of breaking or broken cultures that they no longer give satisfaction, no longer 'make life worth living'" (Oliver La Farge, Foreword to Oscar Lewis, *Five Families* (New York: Science Editions, 1962), pp. ix–x). "There is a common theme apparent in their attitudes and in their actions, every one of them. The theme is a sense of a lack of something in their lives. The new world they have embraced, with various feelings, leaves them with an emptiness, a void that they all recognize and all want to fill" (Colin M. Turnbull, *The Lonely African* (London: Chatto and Windus, 1963), p. 27).

objective determinisms, then we must acknowledge that revolt against the present situation cannot be oriented towards rational, explicit ends until the economic conditions for the formation of a rational consciousness of those ends are fulfilled, in other words, until the prevailing order contains the potentiality of its own disappearance and so produces agents capable of making its disappearance their project.

The sense of honour[1]

When we discuss the levels of descriptive and explanatory adequacy, questions immediately arise concerning the firmness of the data in terms of which success is to be judged...For example...one might ask how we can establish that the two are sentences of different types, or that "John's eagerness to please..." is well-formed, while "John's easiness to please..." is not, and so on. There is no very satisfying answer to this question; data of this sort are simply what constitute the subject matter for linguistic theory. We neglect such data at the cost of destroying the subject.
    Noam Chomsky, *Current Issues in Linguistic Theory*

N. had always been comfortably off. He used to make others work for him, taking the best from their fields and houses as if by seignorial right. Although he had gone down a good deal in the world, he still thought he could do whatever he liked. He felt he had a right to demand everything, speak while others remained silent, insult and even physically assault those who stood up to him. No doubt this is why he was regarded as an *amahbul*. An *amahbul* is the shameless, brazen individual who oversteps the bounds of acceptable behaviour, who assumes an arbitrary power and commits acts that are contrary to what is counselled by the art of living. Men endeavour to avoid *imahbul* (plural of *amahbul*), because nobody wants a confrontation with them; they are immune to shame, and anyone who got into an argument with them would always end up the victim, even if he happened to be in the right.

    N. had a garden wall that needed rebuilding. His neighbour had a retaining wall. N. knocked this wall down and carried the stones into his own garden. For once, the victim of N.'s arbitrary act was not someone weaker than himself but had ample means of self-defence. He was young and strong, had many brothers and kinsmen, and belonged to a large and powerful family. Clearly,

---

1. An earlier English version of this text was published under the title "The Sentiment of Honour in Kabyle Society", in *Honour and Shame*, ed. J. Peristiany (London: Weidenfeld and Nicolson, 1966), pp. 191–241. It was first published in French as "Le sens de l'honneur", in *Esquisse d'une théorie de la pratique* (Paris and Geneva: Librairie Droz, 1972), pp. 13–43.

if he did not take up the challenge, it was not out of fear. And so public opinion could not see this offensive act as a genuine challenge, casting a slur on his honour. On the contrary, both public opinion and the victim affected to ignore it: for it is absurd to get into a quarrel with an *amahbul*. "Keep clear of the *amahbul*", isn't that how the saying goes?

However, the victim went to see the culprit's brother. The latter sided with the complainant but was at a loss how to make the *amahbul* see reason. He made it clear he thought the victim had made a mistake in not reacting immediately with equal violence, and he added: "Who does that wretch think he is?" Thereupon his visitor abruptly changed his tone and said indignantly, "Who do you take *me* for, Si M.? Do you think I'm prepared to have an argument with Si N. over a few stones? I came to see you because I know you are sensible and will understand what I say. I didn't come to ask for payment for the stones." And here he swore by all the saints that he would never accept compensation. "To do what Si N. did, a man must be an *amahbul*, and I'm not going to cast myself into shame [*adhbahadlagh ruḥiw*][2] with an *amahbul*. I just want to point out that that's no way to build a lawful, just house [*akham naṣaḥ*]." And at the very end of the conversation, he added, "Those who have an *amahbul* in the family ought to deal with him before others do." In other words: "You're wrong not to side with your brother in front of me, even if you give him a talking-to in my absence, which is moreover just what I'm asking you to do"[3]

2. For the Kabyle vocabulary of honour, see p. 131. *Bahdel* (a verb) means to cast someone into shame, dishonour him, completely dominate him, beat him hollow, make a laughing-stock of him, in short, to push one's victory beyond reasonable limits. *Bahdel* is more or less reprehensible according to one's opponent and above all according to what he is reproached with. Where an *amahbul* is concerned, a man does not say "I'm afraid he will ridicule me [*bahdel*]" but "I'm not going to ridicule [*adhbahadlagh* – reflexive] myself [*ruḥiw* – myself, my spirit] with him." *Chemmeth* has much the same meaning and is used in the same ways (*ichemmeth imanis*, he dishonours himself).

3. "He who strips his brother strips himself", says the proverb. "He insults himself [that is to say, his brother or his family]: the donkey is worth more than he is" (*Its'ayer imanis, daghyul akhiris*). '*Ayer* (verb) means to point at, to call to account, reveal, denude someone's '*ar* ('*ar*, vulnerability, weak point, that which gives cause for dishonour), to insult. It denotes the symbolic or ritual insults that women hurl at one another (*lam'ayrath*). Examples of *lam'ayrath*: "Your father is a chicken thief", "Your mother goes begging in the mills." As an unfounded accusation, *lam'ayrath* is permitted to women, and is of no consequence; not so for men. Whereas '*ayer* demands a reply, at least on the same level – insult responding to insult – to parry it and leave the other without any reply, *achuwah* is irreparable. *Achuwah* is to cause loss of face, especially among one's own group, by a clumsy, involuntary action; for instance, revealing a

(Aghbala).⁴ To understand the full subtlety of this debate, one needs to know that it brought face to face a man perfectly versed in the dialectic of challenge and riposte and a man who had lived outside Kabylia for so long that he had forgotten the spirit of the tradition. The latter saw the incident as a petty theft by a brother whom he could disown in the name of justice and good sense, without any infringement of family solidarity, and so he reasoned purely in terms of material interest: the wall is worth so much and this person must be compensated. His interlocutor remained astonished that such an educated man could have so misunderstood his true intentions.

One year, in another village, a peasant was robbed by his *khammes* (share-cropper). The thief was an old hand at that trick but this time he had gone too far. After complaints and threats had failed, the matter was brought before the assembly (*thajma'th*). The facts were known to all, and it was superfluous to prove the charge. The *khammes*, seeing he hadn't a leg to stand on, rapidly set about pleading for forgiveness in accordance with tradition, although he also put forward several arguments in his own defence: that he had been cultivating this land for a very long time; that he looked upon it as his own property; that the landlord, an absentee, had no need of the crop; that, in order to please him, he gave him his own figs, which were of better quality, on the understanding that he would recoup later on the quantity; that he was poor, and the owner rich – "rich so as to give to the poor" – and so on, a whole string of excuses intended to flatter the landlord. He uttered the formula "May God forgive me", which, according to custom, ought to bring discussion to an end. But he added:

If I have acted well, praise be to God (so much the better),
If I have erred, God forgive me.

The landlord was infuriated by this formula, though it was a perfectly legitimate and appropriate one, since it reaffirms that

shameful secret in the presence of members of another group, or throwing members of one's own group into confusion. *Achuwah* is more permissible in a man than in a woman (unlike *'ayer*). A person who suffers *achuwah* will confess to it more readily than someone who suffers *'ayer*.

4. The names in brackets signify the places of origin of informants.

even when he makes honourable amends a man cannot be entirely wrong or at least cannot put himself entirely in the wrong, so that he is always a little bit right, just as the other is always a little bit wrong. The landlord wanted a simple "May God forgive me", an unqualified admission of guilt. Whereupon the *khammes* called the assembly to witness: "Fellow creatures, friends of the saints! Do you see this? I praise God and that man there attacks me for it!" And he repeated the same formula two or three times, each time humbling and abasing himself more. This made the landowner more and more furious, so that in the end, despite the respect they felt for an educated man, a stranger to that region, the whole village felt they had to reprove him for his conduct. When tempers had died down, the landlord regretted his intransigence. On the advice of his wife, who was more familiar with local customs, he sought out the village *imam* and some older kinsmen to apologize for his behaviour. He pointed out that he had been a victim of *elbahadla* (the action of *bahdel*), as everyone had realized.

In a third village, a certain incident had aggravated the tension between the two factions (*ṣuf*). One of the factions, weary of this situation, sent a whole delegation to see an important member of the opposing side. The delegation was made up of marabouts from the douar and from neighbouring douars, the village *imam*, all the *ṭulba* (plural of *ṭaleb*) from a neighbouring *thim'amarth* (religious school), more than forty people in all, who were provided with transport, food, and lodging. To everyone in the region – except the person who was the object of the operation, an uprooted Kabyle who was out of touch with the customs – it was clear that this was a ritual. Custom demanded that after kissing the negotiators on the forehead, one should accept their proposals and call for peace. This did not rule out the possibility of reopening hostilities later, on any pretext, without anyone finding cause for complaint. The dignitaries announce the purpose of their visit: "The Ath— come to seek pardon." Custom requires that they should initially dissociate themselves from the faction on whose behalf they have come to intercede. The next to speak, with dignity, are those who ask for pardon "in the interest of all, and especially in the interest of the poorest in the village. For it is they who suffer from our quarrels; they are quite lost, as you can see,

The sense of honour

one cannot but pity them..." (They continue in this vein with similar face-saving reasons.) "Let us make peace and forget the past." The recipient of this entreaty is expected to manifest a certain reluctance and express a few reservations; alternatively, with tacit complicity, part of his faction should stiffen its attitude, while the other, in order to keep negotiations going, should be more conciliatory. In the midst of the discussion, the mediators intervene; their task is to accuse and find fault with the solicited party, so as to restore the balance and save the supplicator from total humiliation (*elbahadla*). For the mere fact that one has appealed to the good offices of the marabouts, fed them, and come with them is in itself a sufficient concession; abasement cannot be taken any further. Moreover, the mediators, being above all rivalries and enjoying a prestige which enables them to impose a settlement, can afford to adopt a slight tone of rebuke towards someone who refuses to give way to entreaties: "To be sure, there may be many wrongs on their side, but you, Si X, have been guilty in this...you ought not to have...and today you must forgive them. Each side forgives the other and we undertake to sanction the peace you are now making, etc." The wisdom of the dignitaries entitles them to apportion rights and wrongs in this way.

But in this particular case, the solicited party, ignorant of the rules of the game, was unable to accept these diplomatic subtleties. He wanted to have everything out, he reasoned in terms of either/or: "What? If you've come to entreat me, it's because the others are in the wrong. They're the ones you must blame, instead of coming and rebuking me. Or are you taking their side because they've fed you and given you money?" No stronger insult could have been thrown at the assembly of notables. As far back as any Kabyle could remember, it was the first time a delegation of such venerable personalities had failed to obtain the agreement of the two parties, and the worst misfortunes were predicted for the offender.

The dialectic of challenge and riposte

A host of similar episodes could be related. But from an analysis of these three stories alone we are able to extract the rules of the game of challenge and riposte. In order for there to be a challenge, the challenger must consider whoever he challenges to be worthy of being challenged, in other words, capable of replying to the challenge. In short, he must recognize his opponent as his equal in honour. To challenge someone is to acknowledge that he is a man, an acknowledgement which is the prerequisite for any exchange and for the challenge of honour insofar as it is the first step in an exchange. It is also to acknowledge him as a man of honour, since the challenge, as such, requires a riposte and is therefore addressed to a man deemed capable of playing the game of honour and of playing it well, which presupposes, first, that he knows the rules and, secondly, that he possesses the virtues needed to comply with them. The sense of equality in honour, which can coexist with actual inequalities, inspires a great number of practices and customs and is manifested particularly in the resistance offered to any pretension to superiority. "I've got a moustache too"[5] is a phrase often used. A braggart is immediately called to order. "Only dung swells", they say. "His head touches his chechia." "Black is black; now it's been tattooed as well!" "He wants to walk like a partridge when he's forgotten how a hen walks!" In the village of Tizi Hibel, in Great Kabylia, a rich family built a European-style family tomb, with a wrought-iron gate, a tombstone, and an inscription, thereby transgressing the convention that tombs should be anonymous and uniform. The day after its completion, the ironwork and headstones had disappeared.

From the principle of mutual recognition of equality in honour, there follows a first corollary: the challenge bestows honour. "The man who has no enemies is a donkey", say the Kabyles, emphasizing not the animal's stupidity but its passivity. There is nothing worse than being ignored: thus, not to salute someone is to treat him like a thing, an animal, or a women. A challenge, by contrast, is "a high point in the life of the man who receives it" (El Kalaa). It is an opportunity for a man to feel he fully exists as a man, to prove his manliness (*thirugza*) to himself and others. The "complete man" (*argaz alkamel*) must be constantly on the alert, ready to respond to the slightest challenge. He is the guardian of honour

5. The moustache, used as a descriptive term to identify age ("His beard is growing", "His moustache is growing"), is a symbol of virility; so is the beard (more so in the past). To express a sense of deep insult, a man would say: "So and so has shaved off my beard" (or "my moustache").

(*amḥajar*), one who watches over his own honour and that of his group.

The second corollary is that he who challenges a man incapable of replying to the challenge, that is, incapable of pursuing the exchange that has been opened, dishonours himself. This why *elbahadla*, extreme humiliation inflicted publicly, in front of others, is always liable to rebound on to the person who provokes it, the *amahbul* who cannot comply with the rules of the game of honour. Even a man who deserves *elbahadla* has an honour (*nif* and *ḥurma*); that is why, beyond a certain threshold, *elbahadla* recoils on to the man who inflicts it. So a man will generally take care not to cast *elbahadla* on his opponent, but will let him cover himself in shame by his own conduct. In this case, the dishonour is irreparable. The phrase used is: *ibahdal imanis* or *itsbahdil simanis* – "he has dishonoured himself" (Aghbala). Consequently, a man who finds himself in a favourable position should refrain from pushing his advantage too far, and should temper his accusations with moderation: "Better that he strip himself than that I should unclothe him" runs the proverb (Djemaa-Saharidj). His opponent, on the other hand, can always try to reverse the situation by driving him to overstep the permitted limits, while making honourable amends. As we saw in the second story, this is done to win over public opinion, which is bound to disapprove of the accuser's immoderation.

The third corollary, the counterpart of the second, is this: only a challenge (or insult) issued by one's equal in honour is worthy of being taken up. In other words, for there to be a challenge, the man who receives it has to consider the man who makes it worthy of making it. An affront from a person of lesser honour rebounds on to its presumptuous author. "A prudent man [*amaḥdhuq*] doesn't commit himself with an *amahbul*." Kabyle wisdom teaches: "Take from *amaḥdhuq* and give to *amahbul*" (Azerou n-Chmini). *Elbahadla* would redound upon the wise man who was reckless enough to respond to the senseless challenge of an *amahbul*; whereas, by refraining from any riposte, he leaves him to bear the full weight of his arbitrary conduct. Similarly, dishonour would recoil on to the man who dirtied his hands in an unworthy revenge. This is why the Kabyles sometimes had recourse to hired killers (*amekri*, plural *imekryen*, literally, one whose services are hired). So it is the nature of the riposte that gives the challenge (or insult) its meaning and even its status as a challenge or insult, as opposed to mere aggression.

The Kabyles had an attitude towards the black peoples which illustrates these analyses perfectly. Anyone who responded to abuse from a Negro, a man of lower status and bereft of honour, or who fought with him, would have dishonoured himself.[6] A folk tale of the Djurdjura region tells how, in the course of a war between two tribes, one side set Negroes upon its opponents, who immediately laid down their weapons. But the defeated tribe preserved its honour whereas the victors were dishonoured in their victory. It is sometimes also said that, to escape blood vengeance (*thamgart*, plural *thimagrat*), one only had to join up with a black family. But this was such dishonourable conduct that no one would do so even to save his life. A local tradition nonetheless has it that an ancestor of the Negro butchers of Ighil ou Mechedal, the Ath Chabane, was a Kabyle who turned butcher in order to escape blood vengeance and whose descendants could therefore only marry blacks (Aït Hichem).

The rules of honour also used to govern fighting. Solidarity required every man to protect a kinsman against a non-kinsman, an affine against a man from another faction (*ṣuf*), a fellow villager, albeit from a rival faction, against an outsider, and a fellow tribesman against a member of another tribe. But honour forbade several men to fight against a single man; and so countless devices and pretexts had to be used in order to renew the quarrel on one's own behalf. Thus the slightest quarrel always threatened to widen in scope. The wars between the factions – political and martial leagues which were mobilized as soon as an incident arose or the honour of the group was attacked in the honour of one of its members – took the form of a strictly regulated game, an ordered competition, which, far from threatening social order, tended to safeguard it by allowing the spirit of emulation, the point of

6. Of a man who takes little thought for his honour, the Kabyles say: "He is a Negro." Negroes do not have and do not need any honour. They were kept out of public affairs; though they might take part in some collective work, they were not entitled to speak in the assembly meetings; in some places they were not even allowed to attend. A tribe which listened to the opinions of a Negro would have covered itself with shame in the eyes of other tribes. Kept outside the community or maintained as clients of great families, they carried on occupations which were considered to be degrading, such as butcher, skin merchant, or travelling musician (Aït Hichem).

The sense of honour

honour, *nif*,⁷ to express itself – in prescribed and institutionalized forms. It was the same with wars between tribes. The fighting sometimes took the form of a thoroughgoing ritual: insults were exchanged, then blows, and the fighting would cease with the arrival of the mediators. During the fighting, the women encouraged their men with shouts and chants exalting the honour and strength of the family. No attempt was made to kill or crush the opponent. The aim was to show that one had the upper hand, usually by a symbolic act: in Great Kabylia, it is said, the fighting came to an end when one side had taken possession of the main beam (*thigejdith*) and a flagstone from the enemy's *thajma'th*. Sometimes the encounter would turn sour: an ill-judged blow might kill one of the participants or the stronger faction might threaten to break into the living-quarters of the rival faction, the last refuge of their honour. Only then would the besieged bring out their firearms, and this was generally enough to bring the fighting to an end. The mediators, the marabouts and wise men of the tribe, would ask the aggressors to withdraw and the latter would depart under the protection of the pledged word, *la'naya*.⁸ No one would have thought of molesting them; that would have been a breach of *la'naya*, a supremely dishonouring offence.

According to an old man of the Ath Mangellat (Great Kabylia), in the tribal wars pitched battles were rare occurrences, and only took place after the elders had held a council to fix the day for the encounter and assign its objectives to each village. Each man fought for himself but shouts of advice and encouragement were exchanged. People from all the surrounding villages looked on and commented on the courage and skill of the combatants. When the stronger side occupied positions from which it could crush its opponents, or had seized possession of a manifest symbol of victory, the fighting stopped and each tribe went home. Sometimes prisoners were taken; they were placed under the protection

7. *Nif* is, literally, the nose, and then the point of honour, self-esteem; *thinzarin* (or *anzaren*, depending on the region), the plural of *thinzerth*, the nostril, the nose, is also used in the same sense (see also n. 11 below).
8. The social function of the marabouts is evident. They supply the way out, the "door" (*thabburth*) as the Kabyles put it, making it possible to end the fighting without dishonour and shame falling on either side. By a sort of bad faith that is indispensable in ensuring its very existence, Kabyle society provides both the imperatives of honour and the detours which enable men to get round them without transgressing them, at least in appearance.

(*la'naya*) of their captors and were generally well treated. When the fighting was over, they were sent home, clad in a new *gandura*, signifying that they were dead men returning to their villages in their shrouds. The state of war (*elfetna*) might last for years. In a sense, the hostilities were permanent. The beaten tribe would be waiting for its revenge and, at the first opportunity, would seize the flocks and shepherds of its enemy. At the slightest incident, at the weekly market for example, the fighting would flare up again.[9] In short, in such a universe nothing was harder to tell apart than the state of peace and the state of war. Sealed and guaranteed by honour, the truces between villages and tribes, like the protection pacts between families, would bring only a temporary cessation of war, the most serious game which honour has invented. Though economic interest might sometimes provide a pretext and also derive profit from it, the fighting had more in common with an institutionalized, regulated competition than with a war in which all available means are brought into play in order to secure a total victory. This is clear from the following dialogue, related by an old Kabyle: "One day someone asked Mohand Ouqasi: 'Are you coming to the war?'

"'What do you do in a war?'

"'Well, as soon as you see a Rumi, you fire a bullet at him.'

"'Just like that?'

"'What do you expect us to do?'

"'I thought you were supposed to argue, then exchange insults, and finally fight each other!'

"'Not at all; he shoots at us and we shoot at him. That's all. Are you coming, then?'

"'No. When I'm not angry I can't shoot at people.'"[10]

But the point of honour had other opportunities, besides war, to manifest itself. It inspired, for instance, the rivalries between the villages, which vied to have the tallest and most beautiful mosque; the most elaborate fountains, best protected from the public gaze; the most sumptuous feasts; the cleanest streets; and so on. All kinds of institutionalized, ritual competitions provided further pretexts for contests of honour, such as the target-shooting

9. In the summer of 1959, an old man in the village of Aïn Aghbel, in the Collo region, gave me a description similar in all respects.
10. "Souvenirs d'un vieux Kabyle: lorsqu'on se battait en Kabylie", *Bulletin de l'Enseignement des Indigènes de l'Académie d'Alger*, Jan.–Dec. 1934, pp. 12–13.

which took place on the occasion of every joyful event – the birth of a boy, a circumcision, or a wedding. At wedding times, the escort of men and women entrusted with fetching the bride from a neighbouring village or tribe had to succeed in two successive contests, the first for the women, two to six "emissaries" renowned for their talent, and the second for the men, eight to twenty good marksmen. The emissaries took part in a poetry contest with the women of the bride's family or village, and were expected to have the last word; it was up to the bride's family to choose the nature and form of the test, which consisted either of riddles or a verse competition. The men vied at target-shooting. On the morning of the escort's departure for home, while the women were preparing the bride and the father was being complimented, the men among the retinue endeavoured to shatter with their bullets fresh eggs (sometimes flat stones) embedded in a slope or a tree trunk at a great distance. If they failed, the bridegroom's guard of honour set off again, covered with shame, after passing under the saddle of a donkey and paying a fine. These games also had a ritual function, as is attested both by the rigorous formalism with which they proceeded and by the magical practices which they occasioned.[11]

Though every offence is a challenge, every challenge, as we shall see, is not an outrage and an offence. For the competition of honour can be situated in a logic very close to that of the game or wager, a ritualized, institutionalized logic. What is then at stake is the point of honour, the *nif*, the will to overcome one's rival in a man-to-man struggle. According to game theory, the good player is one who always assumes that his opponent will be able to find the best strategy and who adjusts his own play appropriately; similarly, in the game of honour, both challenge and riposte imply that each participant chooses to play the game and to comply with the rules while assuming that his opponent is capable of making the same choice.

The challenge, properly so-called, and also the offence, presup-

11. The old witches used various devices to charm the eggs so that they would remain "virgin". To break the spell, the eggs had to be pierced with a needle (see Slimane Rahmani, "Le tir à la cible et le *nif* en Kabylie", *Revue Africaine*, no. 93 (1949), 126–32). In the logic of the ritual system, the rifle and the rifle shot (like the needle) are associated with male sexuality. There is every reason to think that, as in a number of other societies (see for example G. Bateson, *Naven* (Stanford, Calif.: Stanford University Press, 1936), p. 163), the nose (*nif*), the symbol of virility, is also a phallic symbol.

pose, like the gift, the choice of playing a particular game in accordance with certain rules. The gift is a challenge which honours the person to whom it is addressed, at the same time putting his point of honour (*nif*) to the test. In consequence, just as the man who insults someone incapable of riposting dishonours himself, so too does the man who makes an excessive gift, ruling out the possibility of a return gift. Compliance with the rule demands, in each case, that the recipient should be left the chance to respond; in short, that the challenge should be a reasonable one. But, by the same token, a gift or challenge constitutes a provocation, a provocation to reply: "He has put him to shame", the Moroccan Berbers used to say, according to Marcy, apropos of the challenge-gift (*tawsa*) which marked the great occasions. The man who has received the gift or suffered the offence is caught in the toils of exchange and must adopt a line of conduct which, whatever he does, will be a response (even by default) to the provocation constituted by the initial act.[12] He can choose to prolong the exchange or to break it off (see diagram). If, obedient to the point of honour, he opts for exchange, his choice is identical with his opponent's initial choice; he agrees to play the game, which can continue *ad infinitum*: for the riposte is *per se* a new challenge. It is said that in the past no sooner had vengeance been accomplished than the whole family rejoiced at the ending of dishonour, *thuqdha an-tsasa*, that is to say, both relief from the pain the offence had caused them in their "livers", and the satisfaction of the desire to be avenged. The men fired rifle shots and the women uttered cries of "you-you", proclaiming that vengeance had been achieved, so that all might see how a family of honour can promptly restore its prestige and also so that the opposing family should be in no doubt as to the source of its misfortune. What's the use of revenge if it remains anonymous?

12. G. Marcy, "Les vestiges de la parenté maternelle en droit coutumier berbère et le régime des successions touarègues", *Revue Africaine*, no. 85 (1941), 187–211. One of the paradoxes of communication is that one still has to communicate in order to indicate the refusal to communicate; and every civilization has a symbolism of non-communication. For the Kabyles, it is essentially the fact of turning one's back on someone – as opposed to *facing* him (*qabel*), the stance befitting the man of honour – and of refusing to speak ("They don't speak to each other: it's like cat and rat between them"). To express symbolic aggression or provocation, a man will say "I piss on you" (*a k bachegh*), "I piss in your path." The man who does not care about the honour of his family is said to "piss on the tail of his garment". A stronger expression is *edfi*, to soil (literally, to spread cowdung on seedlings so as to keep animals away). A woman challenges or insults other women by "pulling up her skirt" (*chemmer*).

The sense of honour

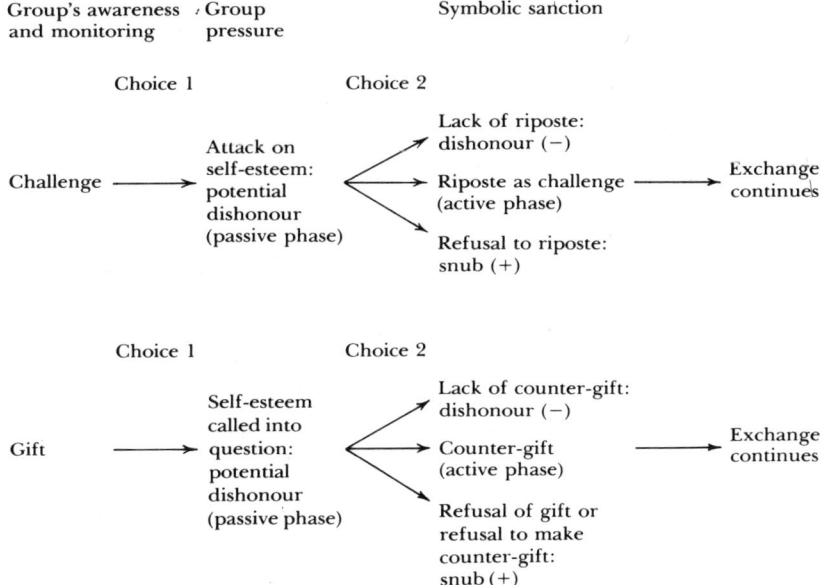

At Djemâa-Saharidj they still remember a *thamgart* that lasted from around 1931 to 1945, in the Ath Khellili tribe (Ath Zellal). "It began like this: two brothers killed two brothers from another family. To make it look as if they had been attacked, one of them wounded the other. They were sentenced to prison, one for eight years, the other for a little less. When the second brother (the most influential in the family) was released, he was always glancing behind him, always on his guard. He was slain by a hired killer. A third brother, who was a soldier, smashed the head of a member of the other family with a stone. The two families threatened to exterminate each other. There had already been eight victims (including the four already mentioned). The marabouts were commissioned to try and settle the dispute. All their peace-making efforts came to nothing, and the third brother, the soldier, was still determined to carry on the struggle. The mediation of a notable from a neighbouring tribe, who had been a caid and was universally respected, was called for. He went to see the obstinate soldier and gave him a stern warning. "Your head is in the *delu* [the funnel which feeds the grain into the mill]; next time, it will go under the grindstone." The young man broke down and offered his head. He was asked to say solemnly that he agreed that the killing should stop. The *fatiha* was pronounced. In the presence of the assembled village, an ox was sacrificed. The young man gave money to the marabouts. And everyone ate couscous together." (The story was told by one of the protagonists.)

It is clear that the group is obliged to intervene when the sub-groups are threatened with extinction. Because the logic of challenge and riposte would extend the conflict *ad infinitum*, it is necessary to find an honourable loophole which casts neither side into dishonour and which allows the imperatives of honour to be suspended in the particular case without being brought into question. The task of conciliation always fell to the group encompassing the two sides or to "neutral" groups, outsiders or marabout families. Thus, so long as the dispute is contained within the bounds of the great family, the wise men dictate the line of conduct and calm the conflict. Sometimes they make a refractory individual pay a fine. When conflict arises between two great families, the other families in the same *adhrum* (clan) endeavour to settle it. In short, the logic of conciliation is the same as the logic of conflict between sections of the lineage, whose first principle is contained in the proverb "I hate my brother, but I hate the man who hates him." When one of the two sides was of marabout origin, other marabouts from outside were brought in to invite them to make peace. The wars between the two factions obeyed the same logic as that of revenge. This is understandable when it is realized that revenge is never, strictly speaking, individual; the avenger is always mandated by the sub-group to which he belongs. The conflict would sometimes go on for decades.

"My grandmother related to me", recounts an informant from Djemâa-Saharidj, aged about sixty, "that the *ṣuf ufella* (the "upper" faction] spent twenty years away from home, in the Hamrawa valley. For it sometimes happened that the defeated *ṣuf* had to take flight with its women and children. In general, the antagonism between the factions was so severe and uncompromising that marriages were impossible. But occasionally, to set the seal on peace between two families or two factions, a marriage was arranged between two influential families. The marriage guaranteed the end of the struggle. In this case there was no dishonour. To seal the peace after a conflict, the two factions met together. The leaders of the two sides brought with them a little gunpowder. This was put into reeds that were then exchanged. This was *aman*, peace."

Choosing the other alternative may take on different and even opposite meanings. The offender may, by virtue of his physical strength, his prestige, or the size and authority of the group he belongs to, be superior, equal to, or inferior to the offended party. Though the logic of honour implies recognition of an ideal equality in honour, the popular consciousness is no less aware of real inequalities. The man who declares "I've got a moustache too" is answered with the proverb "The moustache of the hare is not that of the lion..." Thus one sees the development of a whole spontaneous casuistry, infinitely subtle, which we must now analyse.

Let us take the case where the offended party has, at least ideally, the means of riposting. If he shows himself incapable of taking up the challenge (whether a gift or an offence), if, out of cowardice or weakness, he backs away and declines the possibility of replying, in a sense he chooses to bring dishonour upon himself, and it is then irreparable (*ibahdal imanis* or *simanis*). He declares himself defeated in a game which he ought to have played despite everything. But non-response can also express the refusal to riposte: the recipient of the offence refuses to see it as an offence and by his disdain, which he may manifest by employing a hired killer, he causes it to rebound on its author, who is thereby dishonoured.[13] Similarly, in the case of the gift, the recipient can indicate that he chooses to refuse the exchange either by rejecting the gift, or by immediately or subsequently presenting a counter-gift exactly identical to the original gift. Here too the exchange is at an end. In short, within this logic, only escalation, challenge responding to challenge, can signify the choice of playing the game, by the rule of ever renewed challenge and riposte.

Let us now consider the case where the offender is indisputably stronger than the offended. The code of honour and the public opinion responsible for seeing that it is complied with merely require the offended party to be willing to play the game. Evasion of the challenge is the only blameworthy attitude. In fact it is not necessary for the offended party to triumph over his assailant in order to be rehabilitated in the eyes of opinion. No blame is attached to a loser who has done his duty. Indeed, if he is beaten by the law of combat, he is the victor by the law of honour. Moreover, *elbahadla* recoils on to an aggressor who has also emerged victorious from the confrontation, thereby doubly abusing his superiority. The victim can also cast *elbahadla* back on to his opponent without resorting to a riposte. He only has to adopt an attitude of humility which, by emphasizing his weakness, brings out the arbitrary and immoderate character of the offence. He thus invokes, unconsciously rather than consciously, the second corollary of the principle of equality in honour, whereby he who offends against an individual incapable of taking up the challenge dishonours himself.[14] This strategy is clearly only acceptable on condition that there is no doubt in the eyes of the group as to the disparity between the antagonists. It is appropriate for individuals who are socially recognized as weak, clients (*yadh itsumuthen*, those who lean upon), or the members of a small family (*iṭa'fanen*, the thin, the weak) (Aghbala).

Finally there is the case in which the offender is inferior to the person offended. The latter may riposte, thereby transgressing the

13. Cf. the first story, pp. 95–7. "A family is helpless", say the Kabyles, "if it doesn't include at least one thug." Since the man of honour cannot condescend to take up the insults of an unworthy individual and yet is not immune from such abuse, especially in cities, he needs to be able to send one lout to deal with another.
14. Cf. the second story, pp. 97–8.

third corollary of the principle of equality in honour; but if he abuses his advantage, he exposes himself to the dishonour which would normally have redounded upon the thoughtless offender, a despised (*amaḥqur*) and presumptuous individual. Wisdom advises him rather to abstain from any riposte and to play what we might call the "snub" gambit.[15] He should "let him bark until he is weary of it", and "refuse to vie with him". Since failure to riposte cannot be attributed to cowardice or weakness, the dishonour redounds upon the presumptuous offender.

Although each of the cases which have been examined could be illustrated with a host of observations or stories, usually the differences are never so clear-cut, so that everyone, with group opinion at once his judge and accomplice, can play on the ambiguities and equivocations of conduct. Thus, because the gap between non-response inspired by fear and the refusal to respond as a sign of contempt is often infinitesimal, disdain can always serve as a mask for pusillanimity. But every Kabyle is a master of casuistry, and the court of opinion is always there to judge.

The driving force of the dialectic of honour is therefore *nif*, which inclines men to choose to riposte. But in fact, not only does the cultural tradition offer no possibility of escaping the code of honour, but the moment of choice is precisely the time when the pressure of the group makes itself felt most strongly. First, there is pressure from the members of the family, who are ready to step into the place of any defaulter, because their honour, like their land, is undivided, so that the infamy of one taints all the others. Then there is pressure from the clan or village community, always quick to condemn cowardice or complacency. When a man finds himself obliged to avenge an offence, those about him take care not to remind him of it. But everyone observes his slightest gesture, trying to guess his intentions. All his kinsmen are uneasy until the day he outlines his plans before a family council, assembled at his request or that of the eldest member. Generally they offer to help him, either by giving money to pay for a hired killer, or by accompanying him if he insists on avenging

15. Though all the analyses presented in this chapter constantly refer the Western reader to his own cultural tradition, the differences should not be minimized. This is why, except in cases where they seemed irresistible, I have made it a rule not to suggest comparisons, for fear of encouraging ethnocentric identifications based on superficial analogies.

The sense of honour

himself by his own hand. Custom requires him to reject this assistance and simply ask that, in case of failure, someone else should complete his task. Honour demands that, united like the fingers of the hand, all members of the family should, if necessary, one by one, in order of kinship, undertake the task of vengeance. When the offended person shows less determination and, without publicly renouncing revenge, constantly postpones performing it, the members of the family begin to grow anxious. The wisest among them consult together and one of them is asked to remind their defaulting kinsman of his duty, insisting that he must act. Should this call to order have no effect, threats are resorted to. He is warned that someone else will carry out the revenge in place of the person actually offended; the latter will be dishonoured in everyone's eyes, but will nonetheless be held responsible by the opposing family, and so threatened in his turn with *thamgart* (blood vengeance). Realizing that he is laying himself open to the combined consequences of cowardice and revenge, he is obliged to go out and do his duty, "backwards", as the saying goes, or to opt for exile (Aït Hichem).[16]

The sense of honour is enacted in front of other people. *Nif* is above all that which leads a man to defend, at all costs, a certain self-image intended for others. The "man of worth" (*argaz el'ali*) must constantly be on his guard; he must watch his words, which, "like bullets fired from the rifle, don't come back"; the more so because his every act and his every word commit the whole group. "Animals are fastened by their legs, men bind themselves by their tongues." By contrast, the man of little worth is one of whom people say "*ithatsu*", "he has a habit of forgetting". He forgets his word (*awal*), that is, his pledges, his debts of honour, his duties. "A man of the Ilmayen once said he wished he had a neck as long

16. The cousin of a complaisant husband (called *radhi*, the consenter, or *multa'lem*, he who knows), said to somebody one day: "What do you expect? When you have a brother who has no *nif*, you can't stick a *nif* of earth on him!" And he went on: "If my cousin was an invalid, it would be right for me to avenge him. If he had no money, it would be right for me to pay for him. But he just sits back and takes it, and doesn't care. I'm not going to ruin myself or get sent to Devil's Island for him!" (El Kalaa). The fear of French justice, the weakening of the sense of family solidarity, and the contagion of another value system have led the Kabyles to depart frequently from the old code of honour. In the old peasant society, honour was undivided, like the family land. Alongside the tendency to break up the joint ownership of the family property which has manifested itself more and more strongly in the last twenty years, the feeling has developed that the defence of honour is a matter of purely personal concern.

as the camel's, so that when his words left his heart they would have a long way to go before they reached his tongue, and he would have time to reflect." Such was the importance attached to the promise and the pledge. "The man of forgetfulness", says a proverb, "is no man." He forgets, and he forgets himself (*ithatsu imanis*); another saying is: "He eats his moustache." He forgets his ancestors and the respect he owes them and the respect he owes himself in order to be worthy of them (the Issers).

A man without self-respect (*mabla el'ardh, mabla lahya, mabla erya, mabla elhachma*) is a man who exposes his inner self, with all its passions and weaknesses. The wise man, by contrast, is one who can keep his secret, who shows prudence and discretion at all times (*amresrur, amahruz nessar*, who jealously keeps the secret). Constant watchfulness over oneself is necessary if one is to obey the fundamental precept of the social code which forbids making an exhibition of oneself, and demands that, as far as possible, the innermost personality, with its uniqueness and individuality, should be kept under a veil of modesty and discretion. "Only the Devil [*Chitan*] says 'I'", "Only the Devil begins with himself", "The assembly [*thajma'th*] is the assembly; only the Jew is alone." All these sayings express the same imperative: one which demands the sacrifice and negation of the inner self and is enacted both in the self-effacement required by solidarity and mutual help and in the discretion and modesty of seemliness. The man incapable of self-mastery, who shows impatience or anger, speaks recklessly or laughs without reason, is precipitate or uncontrolled, acts without thinking, throws his weight about, shouts, vociferates (*elhamaq*), in short, gives way to his first impulse, is a man unfaithful to himself, falling short of the ideals of dignity, distinction, and modesty, virtues which are all summed up in one word, *elhachma*. By contrast, the man of honour is essentially loyal to himself, concerned to live up to a certain ideal self-image. Prudent, level-headed, restrained in his language, he always weighs the pros and cons (*amiyaz* as opposed to *aferfer*, he who flits, the "light" man or *achettah*, he who dances); he pledges his word frankly and does not evade his responsibilities with a *wissen*, "perhaps", "who knows?", a reply that is fitting only for women. He is the man who keeps his word, to others and to himself, of whom others say "he is a man and a word" (*argaz d'wawal*) (El Kalaa).

The sense of honour

The point of honour is the basis of the ethic appropriate to an individual who always sees himself through the eyes of others, who has need of others in order to exist, because his self-image is inseparable from the image of himself that he receives back from others. "Man [is man] through men; God [alone]", says the proverb, "[is God] through himself" (*Argaz sirgazen, Rabbi imanis*). The man of honour (*a'ardhi*) is at once the virtuous man and the man of good repute. Respectability, the obverse of shame, is essentially defined by its social dimension, and so it must be won and defended in the face of everyone. Boldness and generosity (*elhanna*) are the supreme values, whereas evil lies in weakness and pusillanimity, in suffering the offence without demanding amends.

So the dynamics of the exchanges of honour are essentially based on the pressure of opinion. He who renounces vengeance ceases to exist for other people. This is why even the man most lacking in "heart" (*ul*) always has enough *hachma* (shame, modesty) to take revenge. The formulae used to express dishonour are significant: "How can I present myself (*qabel*) before other people?" "I won't be able to open my mouth in front of other people." "Won't the earth swallow me up?" "My clothes have slipped from my body." The fear of collective reprobation and shame (*el'ar, lahya, el'ib ula yer medden*), the negative counterpart of the point of honour, is such as to compel even the man most lacking in point of honour to comply, reluctantly but of necessity, with the dictates of honour.[17] In groups whose members are well known to one another, such as the Kabyle village, the pressure of public opinion is exerted at all times: 'He who says the fields are empty (deserted) is himself empty of good sense." Penned within this enclosed microcosm in which everybody knows everybody, condemned without possibility of escape or release to live with other people, under the scrutiny of other people, each individual feels a deep anxiety about "people's words" (*awal medden*), "heavy, cruel, and inexorable" (the Issers). All-powerful opinion is what decides the reality and gravity of an offence; opinion imperiously demands reparation. For example, a thief who enters an inhabited house, as opposed to a thief who steals cereals or animals left outside, lays himself open to blood

17. In Béarn people say of a man who delays in doing his duty: he will have to do it "out of shame or out of honour". In other words, the fear of shame will force on him what the sense of honour cannot inspire in him.

vengeance; this is because people will be quick to insinuate that the honour of the womenfolk has not been respected. Thus the fascinated attention paid to the conduct of others, together with the obsessive fear of their judgement, render unthinkable or despicable any attempt to free oneself from the dictates of honour.

Because every exchange contains a more or less concealed challenge, the logic of challenge and riposte is only the limit towards which every act of communication, and gift exchange in particular, tends.[18] But the temptation to challenge and have the last word is counterbalanced by the need to communicate. A man who puts his opponent to too severe a test runs the risk of having the exchange interrupted. So communication takes place in the compromise between contract and conflict. Generous exchange tends towards assault by generosity; the greatest gift is, at the same time, the one most likely to throw its recipient into dishonour by forbidding any counter-gift. Thus the *tawsa*, a gift presented by the guests on the occasion of the great family feasts and publicly proclaimed, often gives rise to competitions of honour and ruinous outbiddings. To avoid this, an agreement may be made as to the maximum value of the gifts. Similarly, at the time of marriages and circumcisions, the families make it a point of honour to give as sumptuous feasts as possible, at the risk of ruining themselves. This is particularly the case when a daughter is marrying outside her village. There is emulation even between members of the same family, for instance among the women (sisters-in-law, the mother) when a girl marries. I was told that in 1938 in the Ath-Waghlis tribe a man spent more than 3,000 francs when his daughter's first child was born, buying 1,400 eggs, 15 fowl, 300 francs' worth of mutton, 20 kilos of salt meat, 20 kilos of fat, oil, coffee, semolina, 25 garments, etc. Another man in the same tribe, to honour his daughter on a similar occasion, sold his one remaining field. But there is general agreement in denouncing "the Devil's point of honour", *nif nechitan,* or the foolish point of honour (*thihuzzith*) which leads a man to bristle and take offence at trifles, to involve his point of honour in futilities and let himself be carried away

18. Reducing phenomena such as the challenge–riposte dialectic and, more generally, the exchange of gifts, words, or women, to their communication function – if only by transferring schemes and concepts from linguistics or communication theory – means ignoring the structural ambivalence which predisposes them to fulfil a political function of domination in and through performance of their communication function.

The sense of honour

into ruinous outbidding of his rivals. "No one incurs shame if he must lose by it", if he has to ruin himself for the sake of glory (*urits-sathhihad galmadharas*). But although, because it engages the point of honour, exchange always bears within it a latent conflict, the conflict of honour still remains an exchange, as is attested by the clear distinction drawn between the stranger and the enemy. Because it leads the will to communicate with others to be sacrificed to the will to dominate them, the point of honour always contains the risk of rupture; but at the same time, the point of honour is what commits a man to pursuing the exchange with the aim of having the last word.

If the offence does not necessarily bear dishonour within it, this is because it leaves open the possibility of riposting, which is affirmed and recognized in the very act of giving offence. But the dishonour which remains potential so long as there is still the possibility of a riposte becomes more and more real the longer vengeance is delayed. So honour requires the time-lag between the offence and the reparation to be as short as possible. A great family has indeed enough men and enough courage not to have to brook a long delay; known for its *nif*, its sensitivity and determination, it is shielded from offences, since, by virtue of the threat which it always holds out for potential aggressors, it is seen as capable of riposting in the very instant that it is offended. The respect a good family inspires is expressed in the phrase that it can "sleep and leave the door open", or that "its women could walk alone with golden crowns on their heads without anyone thinking of attacking them". The man of honour, of whom people say that he fulfils "his role as a man" (*thirugza*), is always on his guard; and so he is immune from even the most unpredictable attack, and "even when he's away, there's someone in his house" (El Kalaa).

But things are not so simple. It is said that Djeha, a legendary figure, asked when he had avenged his father, replied: "When a hundred years had elapsed." And the tale is also told of the lion who walks with measured stride: "I don't know where my prey is", he said. "If it's in front of me, one day I'll reach it; if it's behind me, it'll catch up with me."

Although every transaction of honour, considered externally and as a *fait accompli*, that is, from the point of view of the outside observer, presents itself as a regulated and rigorously necessary sequence of obligatory acts and can thus be described as a *ritual*, the fact remains that each of its moments, whose necessity is revealed *post festum*, is, objectively, the result of a choice and the expression of a strategy. What is called the sense of honour is nothing other than the cultivated disposition, the habitus, which enables each agent to generate, from a small number of implicit principles, all the lines of conduct consistent with the rules of the logic of challenge and riposte (and no other conduct) by means of unlimited inventions which the stereotyped unfolding of a ritual would in no way demand. In other words, though there is no choice that cannot be accounted for, at least retrospectively, this is not to say that every act is perfectly predictable, like the gestures inserted in the rigorously stereotyped sequences of a rite. This is true not only for the observer but also for the agents, who find in the relative unpredictability of the possible ripostes scope for implementing their strategies. But in fact even the most ritualized exchanges, in which all moments of the action and their unfolding are rigorously prescribed, allows a confrontation of strategies, inasmuch as the agents remain the masters of the *time-lag* between the obligatory moments and consequently are able to act upon their opponents by playing with the tempo of the exchange. We have seen that returning a gift at once, in other words abolishing the time-lag, amounts to breaking off the exchange. Likewise we must take seriously the lesson contained in the parables of Djeha and the lion: the perfect mastery of the *models of the way of complying with the models* which is the definition of excellence is expressed in the play with time which transforms ritualized exchange into a struggle of strategies. Thus, when a marriage is proposed, the head of the family whose daughter is asked for must reply immediately if he refuses, but he almost always delays replying if he intends to accept. By this means he is able to draw out as long as possible the conjunctural advantage (related to his position as the person solicited) which may coexist with a structural inferiority (the solicited family often being of lower rank than the family making the request) and which is concretely expressed in the initial imbalance, progressively reversed, in the gifts exchanged between the two families. In the same way, a skilful strategist can turn a capital of provocations received or conflicts suspended, and the potentiality for revenge, ripostes, or conflicts which it contains,

The sense of honour

into an instrument of power, by keeping hold of the initiative for reopening or even ceasing hostilities.

The point of honour and honour: *nif* and *ḥurma*

If certain families and certain individuals are beyond the reach of the offence which takes the form of an intentional attack upon honour, no one is immune to outrage, the involuntary violation of honour. But the simple challenge to the point of honour (*thirzi nennif*, the act of challenging; *sennif*, by *nif*, I dare you! I challenge you!) is distinct from the offence which assails honour (*thuksa nessar, thuksa laqdhar*, or *thirzi laqdhar*, the act of taking away or breaking respect, *thirzi elḥurma*, the act of casting into dishonour). The Kabyles deride the attitude of the nouveau riche, ignorant of the rules of honour, who, trying to redress a slur on his *ḥurma*, riposted by challenging his adversary to beat him in a race or spread out more 5,000-franc notes on the ground. He was confusing two totally unrelated orders: the order of the challenge, and the order of the offence in which the most sacred values are involved and which is organized in accordance with the most fundamental categories of the culture, those which structure the mythico-ritual system.

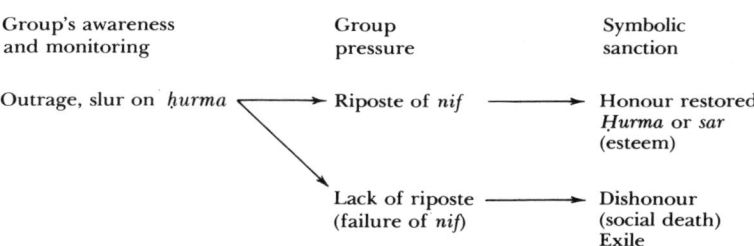

Honour, that which makes the group a target for outrage, is opposed to the point of honour, that by which it can respond to outrage. A clear-cut distinction is made between *nif*, the point of honour, and *ḥurma*, honour, the sum of all that is *ḥaram*, i.e. forbidden, in short, the sacred. Hence what makes the group vulnerable is its most sacred possession. Whereas the challenge touches only the point of honour, outrage is a violation of taboos – sacrilege. An assault on *ḥurma* therefore leaves no room for compromises or evasions. Generally the Kabyles fiercely rejected *diya*, the compensation paid by the murderer's family to the victim's family. A man who accepts it is said to be "a man who has agreed to eat the blood of his brother; for him, only the belly counts" (Aïn Aghbel). *Diya* is accepted only in matters external to *hurma*. Consequently it is the rigour with which it is imposed that distinguishes the interlocking of outrage and revenge from the dialectic of challenge and riposte. Public opinion, the witness and judge, is the sovereign arbiter of both the gravity of the offence and the appropriate revenge. In the case of a slur on *hurma*, albeit committed inadvertently or indirectly,[19] the pressure of opinion is such as to rule out any outcome other than revenge; if vengeance is not forthcoming, the coward devoid of *nif* can only choose between dishonour and exile. If *hurma* is defined as liable to be lost or broken (*thuksa elhurma, thirzi elhurma*, the taking away or breaking of *hurma*), in short, as potential dishonour, then *nif*, without putting *hurma* out of reach of any slur, enables its integrity to be restored. Thus the integrity of *hurma* is a function of the integrity of *nif*. Only the punctilious, active vigilance of the *point of honour (nif)* is capable of guaranteeing the integrity of *honour (hurma)* – which, being the sacred, is, by nature, exposed to sacrilegious outrage – and of winning the *esteem and respectability* which society confers on the man who has enough point of honour to keep his honour safe from offence.

Honour in the sense of esteem is termed *sar*. *Essar* is the secret, prestige, radiance, "glory", "presence". It is said of a man that "*essar* follows him and shines about him", or that he is protected by "the fence of *essar*" (*zarb nessar*). *Essar* shields its bearer against challenges and paralyses would-be aggressors by its mysterious influence, by the fear (*alhiba*) which it inspires. To shame someone is "to take away his *essar*" (another phrase is "to take away *lahya*, respect"). *Essar*, that indefinable thing which makes a man of honour, is as fragile and vulnerable as it is imponderable. "The

19. Since *hurma* is, in a certain respect, identifiable with *haram*, that which is objectively sacred, it can be violated inadvertently. For instance, we have seen that theft from an inhabited house was particularly heinous and demanded revenge because it constituted an attack on *hurma*; theft or fraud in the market only constitutes a challenge and an assault on the victim's self-esteem. The village too has its *hurma*, which can be violated, when, for example, a stranger comes and causes a scandal.

burnous of *essar*", say the Kabyles, "is not tied on; it lies lightly on a man's shoulders" (Azerou n-Chmini).[20]

Ḥurma in the sense of the sacred (ḥaram), *nif*, and ḥurma in the sense of respectability, are inseparable. Thus the more vulnerable a family is, the more *nif* it needs to have in order to defend its sacred values, and the greater are the merit and esteem that opinion accords it. This explains why, far from contradicting or forbidding respectability, poverty only increases the merit of someone who, though particularly exposed to outrage, nonetheless manages to secure respect.

> The following tale, told to me by an aged Kabyle of the Aïth'idel, who had heard it from his father, gives the portrait of the man of honour, a portrait identical in every respect with the one drawn for me by a member of the Issers tribe, which suggests that it concerns a mythical and exemplary figure whose story is always set in a familiar context: "There was once a man named Belkacem u Aïssa who, despite his poverty, was respected for his wisdom and virtue. His influence extended over several tribes. Whenever there was a dispute or a fight, he served as a mediator and settled the conflict. The Ben Ali Cherif, a great family of the region, were jealous of his influence and prestige, especially since he refused to pay them homage. One day, the people of his tribe decided to try and reconcile them. They invited the oldest member of the Ben Ali Cherif family, as well as Belkacem u Aïssa. When the latter entered, the old man, who was already seated, said ironically, 'What fine *arkasen* [plural of *arkas*, the rustic footwear of a ploughman] you have!' Belkacem replied, 'Custom requires men to look others in the face, not look at their feet. It's a man's face, his honour, that counts.' When strangers asked him how he had won his influence over the region, Belkacem answered, 'I first won the respect of my wife, then of my children, then my brothers, then my neighbourhood, then my village; the rest simply followed.'"

Conversely, the point of honour only has meaning and a function in a man for whom sacred things exist, things worth defending. A being devoid of the sacred could dispense with the point of honour because he would in a sense be invulnerable.[21] In short, if the sacred (ḥurma–ḥaram) exists only by virtue of the point of

20. And again: "*Essar* is a turnip seed." The turnip seed is minute and round and extremely slippery. *Essar* also denotes the grace of a woman or girl.
21. The disapproval of celibacy can be understood in terms of this logic. Equality in honour is accompanied by a sort of equality in vulnerability which is expressed, for example, in the phrase often used to rebuke pretentiousness: "Your mother is no better than mine." (This ironic formula should not be confused with the insult "My mother is better than yours" – I surpass you in everything, since I surpass you even here, when in fact every women is as good as another.)

honour (*nif*) which defends it, the sentiment of honour finds its *raison d'être* in the sense of the sacred.

How is the sacred (*ḥurma–ḥaram*) which honour must protect and defend to be defined? Kabyle wisdom replies to this question: "One's house, one's wife, one's rifles." The polarity of the sexes, so strongly marked in this patrilinear society, is expressed in the division of the system of representations and values into two complementary, antagonistic principles.[22] That which is *ḥaram* (i.e., literally, taboo) is essentially the sacred of the left hand, that is, the inside, and more precisely, the female universe, the world of secrecy, the closed space of the house, as opposed to the outside, the open world of the public meeting-place (*thajm'ath*), the world reserved for men. The sacred of the right hand is essentially "the rifles", in other words the group of agnates, the "sons of the paternal uncle", all those whose death must be avenged by blood and all those who are bound to perform blood vengeance. The rifle is the symbolic embodiment of the *nif* of the agnatic group, *nif* in the sense of that which can be challenged and that which enables the challenge to be taken up.[23] Thus the passivity of *ḥurma*, female in nature, is counterposed to the active irritability of *nif*, male in nature. If *ḥurma* is identified with the sacred of the left hand, that is, essentially with what is female, *nif* is the manly virtue *par excellence*.

The opposition between the sacred of the left hand and the sacred of the right hand, in the form of the opposition between *ḥaram* and *nif*, does not, however, exclude complementarity. It is respect for the sacred of the right hand, for the name and renown of the agnatic family, that inspires the riposte made to any offence against the sacred of the left hand. *Ḥurma* is not only that which has value, that which is precious, that which is cherished (*el'azz*), it is what is more precious than that which is most cherished; for sacred value is not the same thing as affective value. The duty to

22. This division, which is in fact one of the fundamental categories of Kabyle thought, particularly of the mythico-ritual system, supplies the fundamental postulates (e.g. the impurity of women) from which the value system builds up its own logic. Here it must suffice to restate those meanings which one needs to know in order to understand the value system which they underpin.
23. Formerly, in certain regions in Great Kabylia, the *thajm'ath* (assembly) required each man of the tribe, under threat of paying a fine, to buy a rifle so as to be able to defend his own and the group's honour. A man who failed to do so, despite the fine, was ostracized, universally despised, and looked upon as "a woman".

The sense of honour 121

defend the sacred imposes itself with the force of a categorical imperative, whether it be the sacred of the right hand, such as a male member of the group, or the sacred of the left hand, such as a woman, a weak, impure, and malignant being. The man of honour carries out revenge and washes away the affront received, regardless of emotion, and in doing so is entirely approved by the group. The Kabyles praise and cite as an example the attitude of Sidi Cherif, the head of a great marabout family of the 'Amrawa, who slew his own guilty daughter, and one still hears the saying: "He has the *nif* of Sidi Cherif." Respect for the sacred of the right hand, for the family honour, is what motivates the taking of revenge for harm done to the sacred of the left hand, the weak side which exposes the group to offence.

Nif is thus loyalty to the family honour, to *ḥurma* in the sense of respectability and esteem, to the name of one's ancestors and the renown attached to that name, to the lineage which must remain unsullied and be protected against offence as against misalliance. The cardinal virtue, the foundation of the whole patrilinear system, *nif* is indeed essentially respect for the lineage of which a man aims to be worthy. The more valorous or virtuous one's ancestors, the more one is entitled to be proud and the more, therefore, one must be punctilious about honour in order to live up to their valour and virtue. The honorability and purity of the lineage impose duties rather than bestow privileges. Those who have a name, people of good stock (*ath la'radh*), have no excuses.

The opposition between *ḥaram* and *nif*, between the sacred of the right hand and the sacred of the left hand, is expressed in various homologous oppositions: between woman, the bearer of maleficent, impure, destructive, fearful powers, and man, invested with beneficent, fertilizing, protective potency; between magic, exclusively the business of women and concealed from men, and religion, which is essentially masculine; between female sexuality, guilty and shameful, and virility, the symbol of strength and prestige.[24] The opposition between the inside and the outside, a form of the opposition between the sacred of the left hand and the sacred of the right hand, is expressed concretely in the sharp

24. The link between *nif* and virility is particularly clear in ritual games, such as the target-shooting which takes place on the occason of the birth of a *boy*, circumcision, and marriage.

division between the women's space – the house and its garden, the site *par excellence* of *haram*,[25] a closed, secret, protected space, away from intrusions and the public gaze – and the men's space – the *thajm'ath* (place of assembly), the mosque, the café, the fields and the market.[26] On the one side is the secrecy of intimate life, entirely veiled in modesty, on the other the open space of social relations, of political and religious life; on one side the life of the senses and the emotions, on the other the life of man-to-man relationships, of dialogue and exchange. Whereas in the urban world, where the men's space and the women's space overlap, intimacy is safeguarded by confinement and the wearing of the veil, in the Kabyle village, where the use of the veil is traditionally unknown,[27] the two spaces are clearly separated. The women's path to the fountain avoids the domain of the men; usually, each clan (*thakkarrubth* or *adhrum*) has its own fountain, in its own neighbourhood or close by, so that the women can go there without the risk of being seen by any man outside the group (Aït Hichem).[28] When this is not the case, the function elsewhere

25. The threshold, the meeting point between two antagonistic worlds, is the site of a host of rites, and surrounded with taboos. In some parts of Kabylia, only kinsmen may cross it. In any case no one crosses it unless invited to do so. The visitor announces his presence with a shout (as in southern France) or by coughing or shuffling his feet. In some regions (El Kseur, Sidi Aïch), custom requires a distant kinsman, or a kinsman related through women (e.g. the wife's brother), to present a symbolic gift, called the "sight" (*thizri*), on entering the house for the first time. The village is another sacred space; it may only be entered on foot.
26. It is said that formerly the women went to the market alone; but they were so talkative that the market went on until the market day of the following week. Then the men came along one day armed with sticks and put an end of the idle chattering of their wives... It can be seen that the "myth" "explains" the present division of space and tasks by invoking the "corrupt nature" of women. When someone wants to indicate that the world is topsy-turvy, he says, "The women are going to market."
27. Traditionally, confinement (*lahdjubia*) and the wearing of the veil were only required in the case of the sheikh of the village mosque (to whom the villagers provided, among other services, a supply of wood and the keep of *thanayamts*, to fetch water), a few marabout families not living on an *azib* (a sort of isolated hamlet), and the heads of certain important families who set apart one of the women of the house (usually the youngest wife) by making her *thanahdjabth* (confined).
28. Each lineage, even at the lowest level, constitutes a potential social group. At moments of conflict, political organization redefines itself in accordance with the relative positions of the parties within the genealogy. Consequently the same logic may assemble very extended groups, that is, all the descendants of an ancestor four or five generations back or even those of a mythical ancestor, that of the tribe for example, and also very narrow groups, such as the extended family or even the restricted family. The *thakkarrubth* or *adhrum* can be defined as the totality of the persons who owe one another blood vengeance and between whom there is no blood vengeance, or who are on the same side when conflict arises.

The sense of honour

performed by a spatial opposition is entrusted to a temporal rhythm, and the women go to the fountain at certain times of the day, nightfall for example; a poor view would be taken of the man who went to spy on them. The fountain is for the women what the *thajm'ath* is for the men. There they exchange news and carry on the gossip which centres essentially on all the intimate matters which the men could not talk about amongst themselves without dishonour and which they only learn about through their wives. The man's place is outside, in the fields or at the assembly, amongst other men; this is something the young boy is taught very early. A man who stays at home all day is suspect. A respectable man must show himself, constantly place himself under the gaze of others, face up to them (*qabel*). Whence this formula, often repeated by the women, in which they hint that men remain ignorant of much of what goes on in the house: "O man, you poor wretch, spending all day in the fields like a donkey at pasture!" (Aït Hichem).

The essential imperative is to veil the whole domain of intimacy. Internal dissensions, failures, and shortcomings must on no account be displayed before a stranger to the group. To the set of interlocking social units corresponds a set of concentric zones of secrecy. The house is the first island of secrecy within the clan or sub-clan; the latter keeps its secret from the village, which is itself closed off in secrecy from the other villages. Within this logic, it is natural that the ethic of woman, situated at the heart of the closed world, should be made up essentially of negative imperatives. "Your tomb is your house", a maxim says. "A woman owes her husband fidelity; her home must be well kept; she must see that her children are brought up aright. But above all, she must preserve the secret of family intimacy; she must never belittle her husband or put him to shame (even if she has every reason to do so and all the necessary evidence), either at home or before strangers. If she did so he would have to repudiate her. She must show contentment even if, for example, her husband is too poor to bring anything back from the market. She must not interfere in the men's discussions. She must have confidence in her husband, and refrain from doubting him or seeking proofs against him" (El Kalaa). In short, since a woman is always "so and so's daughter" or "so and so's wife", her honour amounts to the honour of the

ḤURMA–ḤARAM	NIF
Sacred of the left hand	Sacred of the right hand
Female, femininity	Male, virility
Woman, bearer of maleficent and impure powers	Man, bearer of beneficent and protective potency
Left, twisted	Right, straight
Vulnerability	Protection
Nakedness	Enclosure, clothing
Inside	**Outside**
The preserve of women: house, garden	The preserve of men: assembly, mosque, fields, market
Closed, secret world of intimate life: food, sexuality	Open world of public life, of social and political activities: exchanges
Nature	**Culture**
Wet, water, etc.	Dry, fire, etc.

agnatic group to which she is attached. So she must take care that her conduct does not diminish the prestige and repute of the group in any way.[29] She is the guardian of *essar*.

The man, for his part, must above all protect and veil the secrecy of his house and his intimate life. One's "intimate life" means first of all one's wife, who is never referred to as such, still less by her first name, but always by periphrases such as "the daughter of so and so", "the mother of my children", or "my house". At home, the husband never speaks to her in the presence of others; he calls her by a gesture, or by a grunt, or by the name of her eldest daughter, and shows her no sign of affection, especially in the presence of his own father or elder brother. To utter one's wife's name in public would be a dishonour: it is often said that men who went to register a birth stubbornly refused to give the wife's name. Similarly, schoolboys who willingly gave their father's name were reluctant to give their mother's name, probably for fear of exposing themselves to insults (to call someone by his mother's name is to accuse him of bastardy) or even witchcraft (in magic, it is always the mother's name that is used). A man should never be asked about his wife or sister: this is because woman is one of those shameful things (the Arabs say *lamra'ara*, "woman is shame") that one never mentions without apologizing and adding

29. Everything takes place as if a woman was incapable of really increasing the honour of the agnates but could only keep it intact by her good behaviour and respectability, or destroy it (*ekkes el'ardh*, to take away repute) by her behaviour. What *can* increase the group's honour is alliance, by marriage, with the woman's male relatives.

The sense of honour

hachak, "saving your respect". And also because woman is for man the sacred thing above all others, as is shown by the phrases customarily used in pledging an oath: "May my wife be taboo to me" (*thahram ethmattuthiw*) or "may my house be taboo" (*ihram ukhamiw*) ("if I fail to do such-and-such").

Intimate life includes everything that belongs to nature – the body and all organic functions, the self with its feelings and passions: all these are things which honour requires to be veiled. Any allusion to these subjects, particularly to one's own sexual life, is not only forbidden but virtually inconceivable. For several days before and after his wedding, the young man withdraws into a sort of retreat to avoid meeting his father, which would cause both of them unbearable embarrassment. Similarly, a girl who has reached the age of puberty ties up her breasts in a sort of corset that is buttoned up and lined; and, in the presence of her father or her elder brothers, she stands with her arms folded over her chest (Azerou n-Chmini).[30] A man will not speak to his father or elder brother about a girl or woman outside the family. It follows that when the father wants to consult his son about his marriage, he uses a kinsman or friend as a go-between. A man will avoid entering a café if his father or elder brother is already in there (and vice versa), and especially will not stand with them to listen to one of the wandering singers who recite bawdy poems.

Food, too, must not be spoken of. Guests are never wished a good appetite, but only satiety. Politeness requires the host constantly to invite the guest to help himself to more, while the latter should eat as discreetly as possible. Eating in the street is indecorous and immodest. To eat his lunch in the market, a man retires to a secluded corner. When bringing home meat, a man carries it hidden in a bag or under his burnous. In the meal itself, the emphasis is not on feeding one's body, but on eating together, sharing the bread and the salt, as a symbol of alliance.

Extreme modesty is also the rule in the expression of the feelings, which is always extremely reserved even within the family, between husband and wife and between parents and children. *Hachma* (or *lahya*), the modesty which dominates all relationships,

---

30. The taboo on nakedness is absolute, even in sexual relations. We have seen, too, that dishonour is described as a stripping naked ("he has undressed me, he has taken away my garments, he has stripped me").

even among the family, is essentially a protection for *ḥaram*, for the sacred and the secret (*essar*). A man who talks about himself is absurd or boastful; he is unable to submit to the anonymity of the group, the essential precept of the seemliness which requires the use of the polite "we" or of the personal form, only the context indicating that it is oneself one is talking about.

Other principles stemming from the fundamental oppositions are those governing the division of labour between the sexes and, more precisely, the distribution, between the men and the women, of those activities regarded as honourable or degrading. In general, most of the tasks performed by a woman are considered dishonourable for a man, by virtue of the mythico-ritual division of beings, things, and actions. The Chenoua Berbers may not touch eggs or chickens in the presence of outsiders to the family. They are forbidden to carry them to market to sell them; that is a job for women or children. It is an insult to an Achenwi to ask him if he has eggs for sale. The men can slaughter chickens and eat eggs but only among their family.[31] The same customs, more or less modified, are found in Kabylia. Similarly, a woman may ride on a mule, with her husband leading it by the rein; by contrast, riding on a donkey is shameful. Girls who dishonoured their families were sometimes paraded on the back of a donkey. Another example: it is degrading for a man to carry dung; this is a woman's job. Similarly, carrying water in earthenware jars and carrying wood for heating are tasks for the women. All these dictates of the code of honour which, taken separately, seem arbitrary, appear on the contrary as necessary when reinserted into the whole mythico-ritual system, based on the opposition between the male and the female, of which the oppositions between the sacred of the right hand and the sacred of the left hand, the outside and the inside, fire and water, the dry and the wet, are particular modes.

The same system of values dominates all early education. As soon as the boy has a name, he is looked upon and must look upon himself as a responsible representative of the group. I was told that in a village in Great Kabylia, a boy about ten years old, the last male of his family, went to funerals even in distant villages and

---

31. See E. Laoust, *Etude sur le dialecte berbère du Chenoua comparé avec celui des Beni Menacer et des Beni Salah* (Paris: Leroux, 1912), p. 15.

attended ceremonies with adults (Tizi Hibel). Everything in the adults' behaviour, all the ceremonies and rites of passage, tend to emphasize to the boy his status as a man and also the corresponding responsibilities and duties. The deeds of childhood are very soon assessed in terms of the ideals of honour. The education given by the father or paternal uncle tends to develop *nif* in the child, and all the manly virtues bound up with it – fighting spirit, valour, strength, and endurance. This education, given by men and designed to make men stresses the paternal lineage, the values which have been bequeathed by the male ancestors and which every male member of the group must preserve and defend.

The same mythico-ritual categories would doubtless be found to be the basis, if not of the logic of matrimonial exchanges, then at least of the ideal representation which the agents conceive of them. The earliness of marriage makes sense when it is remembered that a woman, evil by nature, must be placed as soon as possible under the beneficent protection of a man. "Shame is the maiden" (*al'ar thaqchichth*), and the bridegroom is called *seṭṭat laʿyub*, "the veil cast over shames". The Algerian Arabs sometimes call women "Satan's cows" or "the Devil's nets", meaning that they are the initiators of evil. "Even the straightest of them", says a proverb, "is twisted as a sickle." Like a plant which tends to the left, woman can never be straight, only straightened by the beneficent protection of man.[32] Without here undertaking to reconstruct the objective logic of matrimonial exchanges,[33] it may at least be pointed out that the norms which govern them and the rationalizations most often used to justify their "ideal" form, parallel-cousin marriage, are formulated in a discourse structured in accordance with the mythico-ritual categories. The need to safeguard blood purity and keep the family honour intact is the reason most frequently given to justify marriage with the parallel cousin. A young man who has married his parallel cousin is said to have "protected" her; he has acted in such a way that the secret of family intimacy is kept safe. A man who married into his own family, it is often said, can be sure that his wife will strive to safeguard her husband's honour, that she will keep family conflicts secret and

---

32. "A daughter's dignity", says an Arab proverb, "only exists when she is with her father."
33. See Bourdieu, "La parenté comme représentation et comme volonté", in *Esquisse d'une théorie de la pratique*, pp. 71–151, trans. in shortened form in *Outline of a Theory of Practice* (Cambridge: University Press, 1977), pp. 38–71 (translator's note).

not run complaining to her kinsmen. "A woman who is a stranger to your family will despise you. She will think herself of a nobler family than your own. But your cousin, who has the same paternal grandfather as you, will not be able to curse your ancestors" (Aïn Aghbel). Marriage with an outsider is feared as an intrusion; it makes a breach in the protective fence surrounding family intimacy: "It is better to protect your *nif* than to entrust it to others."

The ethos of honour

The system of honour values is enacted rather than thought, and the grammar of honour can inform actions without having to be formulated. Thus, when they spontaneously apprehend a particular line of conduct as degrading or ridiculous, the Kabyles are in the same position as someone who notices a language mistake without being able to state the syntactic system that has been violated. Because the norms are rooted in the category system of the mythic world-view, nothing is harder or, perhaps, more irrelevant than the attempt to distinguish between the area directly and clearly grasped by consciousness and the area buried in the unconscious. A single example will make the point. The man of honour is the man who faces up (*qabel*), who confronts others by looking them in the face; *qabel* also means to receive someone as a guest and to receive him well, to do him honour. A popular etymology which, true or not, is certainly significant finds the same root in the word *laqbayel* (masculine plural), which designates the Kabyles.[34] *Thaqbaylith*, the feminine of the noun *aqbayli*, a Kabyle, designates the Kabyle woman, the Kabyle language, and also, so to speak, the essence of the Kabyle, in other words Kabyle honour and pride. But *qabel* is also to face the east (*elqibla*) and the future (*qabel*). In the Kabyle mythico-ritual system, the east stands in a relation of homology with the high, the future, day, the male, good, the right-hand, the dry, etc., and is opposed to the west and so to the low, the past, night, the female, evil, the left-hand, the wet, etc. All informants spontaneously give as the essential characteristic of the man of honour the fact that he *faces* others, *qabel*; it

34. See A. Picard, *Textes berbères dans le parler des Irjen* (Kabylie, Algeria, 1961), who accepts this etymology.

The sense of honour

can be seen that the explicit norms of behaviour connect with and reflect the deep principles of the mythico-ritual system.

The ethos of honour is opposed, in its very principle, to a universal, formal code affirming the equal dignity of all men and therefore the identity of their rights and duties. Not only do the rules imposed on men differ from those imposed on women, and duties towards men from duties towards women, but also the commands of honour, directly applied to particular cases and varying according to the situation, are in no way capable of being universalized. The same code will dictate contrary conduct depending on the social field. On the one hand there are the rules governing relations between kinsmen and, more generally, all social relationships that are experienced along the lines of kinship relations ("Help your own people, right or wrong"), and on the other hand there are rules applying in relations with strangers. This duality in attitudes stems directly from the basic principle, established previously, whereby the various conducts of honour are only required towards those who are worthy of them. Rather than a court, in the sense of a specialized body responsible for pronouncing decisions in accordance with a system of rational, explicit legal norms, the clan or village assembly is in fact an arbitrating council or even a family council. Collective opinion is the law, the court, and the agent executing the sanction. The *thajma'th*, where all the families are represented, embodies the public opinion whose feelings and values it expresses and whence it draws all its moral force. The punishment that is most feared is ostracism or banishment: those who suffer it are excluded from the collective sharing of meat, from the assembly, and from all collective activities, in short, condemned to a sort of symbolic death. Thus, the *qanun* of Agouni-n-Tesellent, a village of the Ath Akbil tribe, includes, in a total of 249 articles, 219 "repressive" laws (in Durkheim's sense), i.e. 88 per cent, as against 25 "restitutory" laws, i.e. 10 per cent, and only 5 articles concerning the basis of the political system. The customary rule, the product of a jurisprudence directly applied to the particular and not of the application to the particular of a universal rule, pre-exists its own formulation; for the basis of justice is not a rational and explicit formal code but the "sense" of honour and equity. What is fundamental remains implicit, because unquestioned and unquestionable – what is fundamental, that is to say, the totality of the values and principles which the community affirms by its very existence and which underlie the acts of jurisprudence. "That which honour forbids", said Montesquieu, "is forbidden still more when the laws do not forbid it; and that which honour prescribes is demanded still more when the laws do not demand it."

Postscriptum. Although the ultimate basis of the whole economic and symbolic system clearly lies in a mode of production in which the more or less equal distribution of land (in the form of scattered, fragmented smallholdings) and of the instruments of production (which are, moreover, inefficient and stable) necessarily precludes the development of the productive forces and the concentration of capital, the fact remains that the ideological transfiguration of the economic structures in the representations and strategies of honour contributes to the reproduction of the structures thereby consecrated and sanctified. Similarly, though the way in which the (material and symbolic) heritage is handed on is the cause of competition and sometimes conflict between brothers and, more generally, between agnates, there is no doubt that the economic and symbolic pressures working in favour of the non-division of the family patrimony contribute to the perpetuation of the economic order, and hence also of the political order founded on it, which finds its own form of equilibrium in the tension observable at every level of the social structure, from the lineage to the tribe, between the tendency to associate and the tendency to dissociate. When one tries to account for the fact that a social formation remains enclosed within the perfect cycle of simple reproduction, by merely invoking the negative explanations of an impoverished materialism, such as the unreliability and stability of the techniques of production, one is prevented from understanding the decisive contribution which ethical and mythical representations can make to the reproduction of the economic order of which they are the product, by facilitating misperception of the real basis of social existence, that is to say, in very concrete terms, by making it impossible for the interests which objectively always guide economic and symbolic exchanges, even between

The vocabulary of honour

	Honour			Dishonour		Sacred
Point of honour	Honour	Respectability	Action of dishonouring	State of dishonour	Crime against honour	
nif	eṭ'ardh	essar	bahdel	hachma	eṭ'ar	hurma
if	lahya	nur	'ayer	thibhadlith	aṭ'ib	haram
anzaren	riya	thaqbaylith	achuwah	thim'ayrith	elkhazwa	
thirzi nennif	elhachma	thirugza	hachchem	chuha	tikhzi	
	amesrur (adj.)	thirufla	afdhah	elfadhha	lahram	
	amahruz nessar	chi'a		itswa'ayer (adj.)		
	eṭ'ali		Nouns of action	inahcham		
			ababdel			
			elbahadla			
			ahachchem			
			thuksa nessar			
			thuksa laqdhar			
			thirzi laqdhar			
			thirzi elhurma			

brothers, ever to be openly avowed as such and thus to become the explicit principle of economic transactions, and ultimately of all exchanges betwen men.[35]

35. Although, in order to do justice to the complex dynamics of practice, this text may at times appear to autonomize the agents' strategies in relation to the objective structures, the fact remains that the principle underlying the production of strategies (the habitus) is itself the product of the objective structures; and to succeed in and with their strategies the agents must constantly adjust them to the objective structures. The foregoing analyses of the strategies with which the Kabyle peasants strive to maintain and increase their capital of honour are an inseparable part of a reconstruction of the system of the objective regularities and the material and symbolic stakes of the political and economic game: reinserted in this context, or, more precisely, in the context of the system of reproduction strategies, the practices of honour reveal their function as strategies intended to reproduce symbolic capital, which they fulfil in the reproduction of an economic and political order of which the ethos of honour, the principle generating such strategies, is itself the product.

The Kabyle house or the world reversed[1]

"Man is the lamp of the outside, woman the lamp of the inside."

The interior of the Kabyle house is rectangular in shape and divided into two parts, at a point one-third of the way along its length, by a small openwork wall half as high as the house. The larger of the two parts, approximately fifty centimetres higher and covered with a layer of black clay and cowdung which the women polish with a stone, is reserved for human use. The smaller part, paved with flagstones, is occupied by the animals. A door with two wings provides access to both rooms. On top of the dividing wall are kept, at one end, the small earthenware jars or esparto-grass baskets used to store the provisions kept for immediate consumption, such as figs, flour, and leguminous plants, and at the other end, near the door, the water jars. Above the stable is a loft where, next to all kinds of tools and implements, quantities of hay and straw to be used as animal fodder are piled up; it is here that the women and children usually sleep, especially in winter.[2] Against the gable wall, known as the wall (or, more precisely, the "side") of the upper part or of the *kanun*, stands a brickwork construction in the recesses and holes of which the kitchen utensils (the ladle, the cooking-pot, the dish used to cook wheatcake – *aghrum* – and other earthenware objects blackened by the fire) are kept and at each end of which are placed large jars

1. This text was first published in *Echanges et communications: mélanges offerts à Claude Lévi-Strauss à l'occasion de son 60e anniversaire*, ed. J. Pouillon and P. Marande (Paris and the Hague: Mouton, 1970), pp. 739–58, and reprinted in P. Bourdieu, *Esquisse d'une théorie de la pratique* (Paris and Geneva: Librairie Droz, 1972).
2. The place for sleep and sexual relations seems to vary, but only within the "dark part" of the house. The whole family may sleep in the loft, particularly in winter, or only women without husbands (widows, divorced women, etc.) and the children; or the family may sleep next to the wall of darkness; or the man may sleep on the upper part of the dividing wall, the woman going to bed on the lower part, near the door, but joining her husband in the darkness.

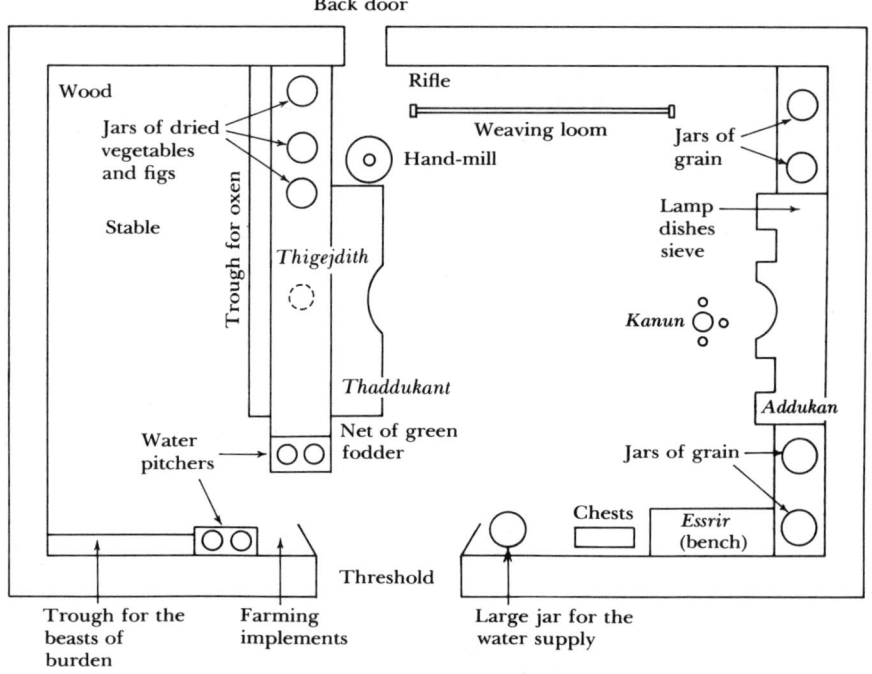

Fig. 1. Plan of the house

filled with grain. In front of this construction is the fireplace, a circular hollow three or four centimetres deep at its centre, around which, arranged in a triangle, are three large stones to hold the cooking utensils.[3]

3. All previous descriptions of the Berber house, even the most precise and methodical ones (such as R. Maunier's, "Le culte domestique en Kabylie" and "Les rites de la construction en Kabylie", in *Mélanges de sociologie nord-africaine* (Paris: Alcan, 1930), pp. 120–77) or those richest in detail concerning the internal organization of space (such as those by E. Laoust, *Mots et choses berbères* (Paris: Challamel, 1920), pp. 50–3, and *Etude sur le dialecte berbère du Chenoua comparé avec celui des Beni Manacer et des Beni Sala* (Paris: Leroux, 1912), pp. 12–15, and H. Genevoix, *L'habitation kabyle* (Fichier de documentation berbère, no. 46, Fort National, 1955)), for all their meticulousness, contain systematic lacunae, particularly as regards the location and orientation of things and activities, because they never look upon the objects and actions as parts of a symbolic system. It is necessary to postulate that each of the phenomena observed derives its necessity and its meaning from its relationship with all the others. This alone enables one to carry out the sorts of observation and questioning that are capable of bringing out the facts which escape any unsystematic observation and which the informants are unable to provide spontaneously because they take them for granted. This postulate is validated by the very findings of the research which it makes possible: the special position of the house within the system of magical representations and ritual practices justifies the initial abstraction by which it is taken out of the larger system so as to be treated as a system in its own right.

The Kabyle house

In front of the wall facing the door, generally referred to by the same name as the outside wall that is seen from the rear courtyard (*tasga*),[4] or else called the weaving-loom wall or the facing wall (one faces it on going in) stands the weaving loom. The opposite wall, where the door is, is called the wall of darkness, or the wall of sleep, the maiden, or the tomb;[5] a bench wide enough for a mat to be spread out on it is set against this wall. This is the place set aside for the festal sheep or small calf, sometimes for the wood or the water pitcher. Clothes, mats, and blankets are hung, in the daytime, on a peg or a wooden crossbar next to the wall of darkness, or else they are put under the dividing bench. Thus, the *kanun* wall is opposed to the stable as the high to the low (*adaynin*, stable, comes from the root *ada*, the bottom), and the weaving-loom wall is opposed to the door wall as the light to the dark. One might be tempted to give a purely technical explanation of these oppositions, since the weaving-loom wall, facing the door, which itself faces eastward, is the most brightly lit and the stable is indeed at a lower level than the rest (the house usually being built at a right angle to the contour lines, to facilitate the drainage of animal waste and dirty water). However, a number of indices suggest that these oppositions are the centre of a cluster of parallel oppositions the necessity of which never stems entirely from technical imperatives and functional requirements.[6]

The dark, nocturnal, lower part of the house, the place for things that are damp, green, or raw – jars of water placed on the benches on either side of the stable entrance or next to the wall of darkness, wood, green fodder – and also the place for natural beings – oxen

---

4. With this one exception, the walls are designated by two different names, according to whether they are considered from the outside or the inside. The outside is plastered over with a trowel by the men, whereas the inside is whitewashed and hand-decorated by the women. This opposition between the two points of view is, as we shall see, a fundamental one.
5. It is said of a father with many daughters: "He has evil days in store for him." Other sayings: "The maiden is the dusk", "The maiden is the wall of darkness."
6. The setting of the house in geographical space and social space, and also its internal organization, are one of the loci where symbolic or social necessity is articulated with technical necessity. This is a case where the principles of the symbolic organization of the world cannot be implemented freely but have, as it were, to come to an arrangement with external constraints, those of technique, for example, which require the house to be built perpendicular to the contours and facing the rising sun (or, in other cases, those of the social structure, which require every new house to be built in a particular locality, defined by genealogy). It is, perhaps, in such cases that the symbolic system reveals its full capacity to reinterpret, in terms of its own logic, the data supplied to it by other systems.

and cows, donkeys and mules – natural activities – sleep, sexual intercourse, childbirth, and also death – is opposed, as nature to culture, to the light-filled, noble, upper part: this is the place for human beings and especially the guest, for fire and objects made with fire, such as the lamp, kitchen utensils, the rifle – a symbol of the male point of honour (*nif*) which protects female honour (*ḥurma*) – and the loom, the symbol of all protection; and it is also the site of the two specifically cultural activities performed within the house, weaving and cooking. These relations of opposition are expressed through a whole set of convergent indices which both establish them and receive their meaning from them. A guest who is to be honoured is invited to sit in front of the weaving loom (the verb *qabel*, to honour, also means, as we have seen, to face up to a person and to face the east).[7] When a man has been badly received, he will say: "He made me sit beside his wall of darkness, as in a grave." The wall of darkness is also called the invalid's wall, and the phrase "to keep to the wall" means to be ill and, by extension, idle: a sick person's bed is in fact placed next to this wall, especially in winter. The connection between the dark part of the house and death is also shown in the fact that the washing of the dead takes place at the entrance to the stable.[8] It is traditionally said that the loft, which is made entirely of wood, is supported by the stable as the corpse is carried by the bearers; *thaʿrichth* designates both the loft and the stretcher which is used

7. The opposition between the part reserved for receiving guests and the more intimate part (an opposition also found in the nomad's tent, which is divided by a curtain into two parts, one open to guests and the other reserved for the women) is expressed in ritual forecasts such as the following: when a cat, a beneficent animal, enters the house with a feather in its fur, or a thread of white wool, if it goes towards the hearth, this portends the arrival of guests, who will be given a meal with meat; if it goes towards the stable, this means that cow will be bought, if the season is spring, or an ox if it is ploughing time.

8. The homology between sleep and death is explicitly stated in the precept that on going to bed one should first lie for a moment on one's right side and then on one's left, because the first position is that of the dead in the tomb. The funeral chants represent the grave, "the house underground", as an inverted house (white/dark, high/low, adorned with paintings/crudely dug out). In doing so they make use of homonymies such as the following, associated with a similarity in shape: "I found people digging a grave,/With their pickaxes they carved out the walls,/They were making benches [*thiddukanin*],/With mortar below the mud" – so runs a chant sung at wakes (see Genevoix, *L'habitation kabyle*, p. 27). *Thaddukant* (plural *thiddukanin*) designates the bench set against the dividing wall, opposite the one against the gable wall (*addukan*), and also the bank of earth on which a dead man's head rests in the grave (the slight hollow in which a dead woman's head is laid is called *thakwath*, as are the small recesses in the walls of the house, in which small objects are kept).

The Kabyle house

to carry the dead. It is clear why a guest cannot, without offence, be invited to sleep in the loft, which is opposed to the weaving-loom wall in the same way as is the wall of the tomb.

It is also in front of the loom wall, facing the door, in full daylight, that the young bride is made to sit, as if to be shown off, like the decorated plates that hang there. When one knows that a baby girl's umbilical cord is buried behind the loom, and that, to protect a maiden's virginity, she is made to step through the warp, from the side facing the door to the side next to the loom wall, then the function of magical protection attributed to the loom becomes evident.[9] Indeed, from the standpoint of her male kin, the girl's whole life is in a sense summed up in the successive positions she symbolically occupies vis-à-vis the weaving loom, the symbol of male protection.[10] Before marriage she is placed behind the loom, in its shadow, under its protection, just as she is kept under the protection of her father and brothers; on her wedding day she is seated in front of the loom, with her back to it, with the light upon her, and thereafter she will sit weaving, with her back to the wall of light, behind the loom. The bridegroom is called "the veil cast over shames", the male point of honour being the sole protection for female honour or, more accurately, the only "fence" against the shame the threat of which is contained in every woman ("Shame is the maiden").[11]

The low, dark part of the house is also opposed to the upper part as the female to the male. Not only does the division of labour between the sexes (based on the same principle of division as the organization of space) give the woman responsibility for most of the objects belonging to the dark part of the house, the carrying of water, wood, and manure, for instance;[12] but the opposition

9. Amongst the Arabs, to perform the magic rite supposed to render women unfit for sexual relations, the betrothed girl is made to step through the slackened warp on the loom, from the outside towards the inside, that is, from the centre of the room towards the wall next to which the weavers sit and work. The same operation, in the opposite direction, undoes the charm (see W. Marçais and A. Guiga, *Textes arabes de Takrouna* (Paris: Leroux, 1925), p. 395).
10. Laoust derives from the root *zett* (to weave) the word *tazettat*, which, among the Berbers of Morocco, designates the protection given to every person travelling in foreign territory or the payment the protector receives in return for his protection (*Mots et choses berbères*, p. 126).
11. See above, pp. 95–132.
12. When a new pair of oxen are first taken into the stable, they are received and led in by the mistress of the house.

between the upper part and the lower part reproduces, within the internal space of the house, the opposition between the inside and the outside, between female space – the house and its garden, the place *par excellence* of ḥaram, i.e. the sacred and forbidden – and male space. The lower part of the house is the place of the most intimate secret within the world of intimacy, that is, the place of all that pertains to sexuality and procreation. More or less empty during the daytime, when all the (exclusively feminine) activity in the house is centred on the fireplace, the dark part is full at night, full of human beings and also full of animals, since the oxen and cows, unlike the mules and donkeys, never spend the night outdoors; and it is never fuller, so to speak, than in the wet season, when the men sleep indoors and the oxen and cows are fed in the stable.

There is a more direct way of establishing the relationship which links the fertility of humans and of the fields with the dark part of the house, a privileged instance of the relation of equivalence between fertility and the dark, the full (or the process of swelling) and the damp, which recurs throughout the mythico-ritual system. Whereas the grain intended for consumption is, as we have seen, kept in large earthenware jars next to the wall of the upper part, on either side of the fireplace, the grain kept for sowing is stored in the dark part of the house, either in sheepskins or wooden chests placed at the foot of the wall of darkness, sometimes under the conjugal bed; or else in chests placed under the bench against the dividing wall, where the woman, who normally sleeps at a lower level, by the stable entrance, comes to join her husband. When one knows that birth is always the rebirth of an ancestor, since the life circle (which should be called the *cycle of generation*) is completed every three generations (a proposition which cannot be demonstrated here),[13] it can be understood how the dark part of the house can simultaneously and without contradiction be the place of death and of procreation, or birth as resurrection.[14]

13. See Bourdieu, *Outline of a Theory of Practice* (Cambridge: University Press, 1977), p. 155.
14. House building, which always takes place when a son is married and which symbolizes the birth of a new family, is forbidden in May, as is marriage. The transporting of the beams, which, as we shall see, are identified with the master of the house, is called *tha'richth*, like the loft and like the stretcher used to carry a corpse or a wounded animal that has to be slain far from the house. It occasions a social ceremony exactly similar in its meaning to that of burial. By virtue of its imperative character, the ceremonial

But this is not all: at the centre of the dividing wall, between "the house of the human beings" and "the house of the animals", stands the main pillar, supporting the "master beam" and the whole framework of the house. Now, the master beam (*asalas alemmas*, a masculine term), which connects the gables and extends the protection of the male part of the house to the female part, is explicitly identified with the master of the house, whereas the main pillar, a forked tree trunk (*thigedjith*, a feminine term) upon which it rests, is identified with the wife (the Beni Khellili call it *Mas'uda*, a feminine first name which means "the happy one"), and their interlocking symbolizes sexual union (represented in the wall paintings, in the form of the union of the beam and the pillar, by two superimposed forked shapes.[15] The main beam, supporting the roof, is identified with the protector of the family honour; offerings are often made to it and it is around this beam that, above the fireplace, the snake, the "guardian" of the house, is coiled. Symbolizing the fertilizing potency of man and also death followed by resurrection, the snake is sometimes represented (in the Collo region, for example) on the earthenware jars made by the women and containing the seedcorn. The snake is also said to descend sometimes into the house, into the lap of a sterile woman, calling her "mother", or to coil itself around the central pillar, growing longer by the length of a coil each time it takes suck.[16] In Darna, according to René Maunier, a sterile woman ties her girdle to the central beam; the foreskin and the reed that has been used for circumcision are hung from the same beam; if the beam is heard to crack those present hasten to say "May it be for the good", because this portends the death of the head of the family. When a son is born, the wish is made that "he may

form it assumes and the extent of the group it mobilizes, this collective task (*thiwizi*) has no equivalent other than burial. As much *hasana* (merit) accrues from taking part in the carrying of the beams, a pious act always performed without remuneration, as from taking part in the collective activities connected with funerals (digging the grave, extracting the stone slabs or transporting them, helping to carry the coffin or attending the burial).

15. See M. Dewulder, "Peintures murales et pratiques magiques dans la tribu des Ouadhias", *Revue Africaine*, 1954, pp. 14–15.
16. On the day of *tharurith wazal* (8 April in the Julian calendar), a decisive turning point in the farming year between the wet season and the dry season, the shepherd goes out very early in the morning and draws water which he sprinkles on the central beam. At harvest time, the last sheaf, cut in accordance with a special ritual (or a double ear of corn), is hung from the central beam, where it remains all year.

be the master beam of the house", and when he has completed the ritual fast for the first time, he takes his first meal on the roof, that is, on the central beam (in order, so it is said, that he may be able to carry beams).

A number of riddles and sayings explicitly identify woman with the central pillar. A young bride is told: "May God make you the pillar firmly planted in the middle of the house." Another riddle says: "She stands upright but has no feet." This fork open upwards and not set on its feet is female nature, fertile, or rather, capable of being fertilized.[17] Against the central pillar the leather bottles full of corn, *hiji*, are piled up and here the marriage is consummated.[18] Thus this symbolic summary of the house, the union of *asalas* and *thigedjith*, which extends its fertilizing protection over all human marriage, is, in a sense, the primordial marriage, the marriage of the ancestors, which, like ploughing, is also the marriage of the sky and the earth. "Woman is the foundations, man the master beam", says another proverb. *Asalas*, defined in a riddle as "born in the earth and buried in the sky", fertilizes *thigedjith*, which is rooted in the soil, the place of the ancestors, the masters of all fertility, and open towards the sky.[19]

Thus the house is organized in accordance with a set of homologous oppositions – fire: water:: cooked: raw:: high: low:: light: dark:: day: night:: male: female:: *nif*: *ḥurma*:: fertilizing: able to be fertilized:: culture: nature. But the same oppositions also exist between the house as a whole and the rest of the universe. Considered in relation to the external world – the male world of public life and farming work – the house, the universe of the women, the

17. A young bride who adapts well to her new house is praised with the expression *tha'mmar*, meaning (among other things – see n. 30 below) "she is full" and "she fills".
18. Among the Berbers of the Aurès, the consummation of marriage takes place on a Monday, a Thursday, or a Saturday, which are *dies fasti*. The day before, the maidens of the bridegroom's family pile up *hiji* against the central pillar – six leather bottles dyed red, green, yellow, and violet (representing the bride) and a seventh, white one (the bridegroom), all of which are filled with corn. At the base of *hiji*, an old woman throws salt to drive away evil spirits, plants a needle in the ground to increase the bridegroom's virility and lays down a mat, turned towards the east, which will be the couple's bed for a week. The women of the bride's family perfume *hiji*, while her mother (just as is done at the start of ploughing) throws a shower of dates into the air, which the children scramble for. The next day, the bride is carried to the foot of *hiji* by a close kinsman of the groom, and her mother again throws flour, dates, swollen wheat, sugar, and honey.
19. In certain regions the ploughshare is placed in the fork of the central pillar with its point turned towards the door.

world of intimacy and secrecy, is *haram*, that is to say, both sacred and illicit for any man who is not a part of it (hence the expression used in swearing an oath: "May my wife [or, my house] become illicit [*haram*] for me if..."). As the place of the sacred of the left hand, *hurma*, with which all the properties associated with the dark part of the house are bound up, it is placed in the safekeeping of the male point of honour (*nif*) just as the dark part of the house is placed under the protection of the master beam. Every violation of the sacred space therefore takes on the social meaning of sacrilege. Thus, theft from an inhabited house is treated in customary law as a heinous act – an offence against the *nif* of the head of the family and an outrage upon the *hurma* of the house and consequently the *hurma* of the whole community.[20]

The woman can only be said to be shut up in the house if it is also pointed out that the man is kept out of it, at least in the daytime.[21] As soon as the sun has risen, in summer he must be out in the fields or at the assembly house; in winter, if he is not in the fields, he must be in the assembly place or on the benches set in the shelter of the pent-roof over the door to the courtyard. Even at night, at least in the dry season, the men and the boys, as soon as they have been circumcised, sleep outside the house, either near the haystacks, on the threshing floor, beside the shackled mule and donkey, or on the fig-drying floor, or in the fields, or more rarely in the *thajma'th*. A man who spends too much time at home in the daytime is suspect or ridiculous: he is "a house man", who "broods at home like a hen at roost". A self-respecting man must offer himself to be seen, constantly put himself in the gaze of others, confront them, face up to them (*qabel*). He is a man among men (*argaz yer irgazen*).[22] Hence the importance attached to the games of honour, a sort of theatrical performance, played out in front of others – informed spectators who know the text and all the stage

20. A guest gives the mistress of the house a sum of money called "the sight". This happens not only when a guest is invited into the house for the first time but when, on the third day of a marriage, a visit is paid to the bride's family.
21. The duality of rhythm related to the division between the dry season and the wet season manifests itself, *inter alia*, in the domestic order. Thus in summer the opposition between the lower part and the higher part of the house takes the form of the opposition between the house proper, where the women and children retire to bed and where the stores are kept, and the courtyard where hearth and hand-mill are set up, meals are eaten, and feasts and ceremonies take place.
22. Relations between men must be established outdoors: "Friends are outdoor friends, not *kanun* friends."

business and are able to appreciate the slightest variations. It is understandable that all biological activities, sleeping, eating, procreating, should be banished from the specifically cultural universe and relegated to the house, the sanctuary of intimacy and the secrets of nature, the world of woman, who is consigned to the management of nature and excluded from public life.[23] In contrast to man's work, which is performed outdoors, woman's work is essentially obscure and hidden ("God conceals it"): "Inside the house, woman is always on the move, she bustles like a fly in whey; outside the house, nothing of her work is seen." Two very similar sayings define woman's estate as that of one who can know no other abode than the house, a tomb above the ground, and the tomb, a house underground. "Your house is your tomb", "Woman has but two dwellings, the house and the tomb."

Thus, the opposition between the house and the men's assembly, between private life and public life, or, if you will, between the full light of day and the secrecy of night, corresponds exactly to the opposition between the dark, nocturnal, lower part of the house and the noble, brightly lit, upper part.[24] The opposition between the external world and the house only takes on its full significance when it is seen that one of the terms of this relation, i.e. the house, is itself divided in accordance with the same principles that oppose it to the other term. So it is both true and false to say that the external world is opposed to the house as the male to the female, day to night, fire to water, etc., since the second term in each of these oppositions divides each time into itself and its opposite.[25]

In short, the most apparent opposition – male (or day, fire, etc.)/female – is liable to mask the opposition male/(male-female/female-female) and, consequently, the homology male/female:: male-female/female-female. It can be seen from this that the first opposition is only a transformation of the second, pre-

23. "The hen does not lay eggs in the market", as a saying puts it.
24. The opposition between the house and the *thajma'th* is seen clearly in different designs of the two buildings. Whereas the house is entered by the door in the front wall, the assembly building takes the form of a long covered passage, completely open at the two gables, and which is crossed from one side to the other.
25. This structure is also found in other areas of the mythico-ritual system. The day is divided into night and day, but the day is itself divided into a diurnal-diurnal part (morning) and a nocturnal-diurnal part (evening). The year is divided into a dry season and a wet season, but the dry season is made up of a dry-dry part and a wet-dry part. A similar structure is observed in the political order, expressed in the saying: "My brother is my enemy, my brother's enemy is my enemy."

supposing a change in the system of reference, whereby the female-female ceases to be opposed to the male-female and, instead, the whole which they make up is opposed to a third term: male-female/female-female $\rightarrow$ female (= male-female + female-female)/male.

The house, a microcosm organized by the same oppositions and the same homologies which order the whole universe, stands in a relation of homology with the rest of the universe. But, from another point of view, the world of the house taken as a whole stands in a relation of opposition to the rest of the world, an opposition whose principles are none other than those which organize both the internal space of the house and the rest of the world and, more generally, all areas of existence. Thus, the opposition between the world of female life and the world of the city of men is based on the same principles as the two systems of oppositions which it opposes to one another. It follows from this that the application to opposed areas of the same *principium divisionis* which establishes their opposition ensures economy and a surplus of consistency, without involving confusion between those areas. The structure $a:b::b_1:b_2$ is doubtless one of the simplest and most powerful that a mythico-ritual system could use, since it cannot counterpose without simultaneously uniting, and is capable of integrating an infinite number of data into a single order by the endlessly repeated application of the same principle of division. It also follows that each of the two parts of the house (and, by the same token, each of the objects that are put there and each of the activities carried on there) is, in a sense, qualified at two degrees, that is, first as female (nocturnal, dark) insofar as it belongs to the universe of the house, and secondly as male or female insofar as it belongs to one or the other of the divisions of that universe. Thus, for example, when a proverb says "Man is the lamp of the outside, woman the lamp of the inside", this must be taken to mean that man is the true light, the light of day, and woman the light of darkness, a dark light; and we know from other sources that woman is to the moon as man is to the sun. Similarly, by her work on wool, woman produces the beneficent protection of weaving, whose whiteness symbolizes happiness;[26]

---

26. "White days" are happy days. One function of the marriage rites is to make the woman "white" (sprinkling of milk, etc.).

the weaving loom, the instrument *par excellence* of female activity, which stands facing the east like the plough, its male homologue, is at the same time the east of the internal space so that, within the system of the house, it has a male value as a symbol of protection. Again, the hearth, the navel of the house (which is itself identified with the belly of a mother), where the embers smoulder with a secret, hidden, female fire, is the domain of the woman of the house, who is invested with total authority in all matters concerning cooking and the management of the food stores;[27] she takes her meals by the fireside, whereas the man, turned towards the outside, eats in the middle of the room or in the courtyard. However, in all the rites in which they play a part, the fireplace and the stones surrounding it derive their magical power, whether to give protection from the evil eye or illness or to bring fine weather, from the fact that they belong to the order of fire, the dry, and the heat of the sun.[28] The house itself is endowed with two-fold significance: though opposed to the public world as nature to culture, it is also, from another standpoint, culture; it is said of the jackal, the embodiment of wild nature, that he builds no home.

The house and, by extension, the village,[29] the full country (*la'mmara* or *thamurth i'amaran*), the precinct peopled with men, are opposed in one respect to the fields empty of men which are called *lakhla*: empty, sterile space. Thus, according to Maunier, the inhabitants of Taddertel-Djeddid believed that those who build their houses outside the village precincts run the risk of their family dying out; the same belief is found elsewhere and the only exceptions are made for the garden, even when remote from the

27. The blacksmith is the man who, like woman, spends his day indoors, beside the fire.
28. The hearth is the site of a number of rites and the object of taboos which make it the opposite of the dark part of the house. For example, it is forbidden to touch the ashes during the night, to spit into the fireplace, to spill water or to weep tears there (Maunier). Likewise, those rites which aim to bring about a change in the weather and are based on an inversion make use of the opposition between the wet part and the dry part of the house. For example, to change the weather from wet to dry, a wool-packing comb (an object made with fire and associated with weaving) and a glowing ember are left on the threshold overnight; conversely, to change from dry to wet weather, the wool-packing and carding combs are sprinkled with water on the threshold during the night.
29. The village also has its *ḥurma*, which all visitors must respect. Just as one must take one's shoes off before going into a house or a mosque or on to a threshing floor, so one must dismount and set one's feet on the ground when entering a village.

The Kabyle house

house (*thabḥirth*), the orchard (*thamazirth*), or the fig-dryer (*tarḥa*), all of which are places which are in some way linked with the village and its fertility. But the opposition does not exclude the homology between the fertility of humans and the fertility of the field, each of which is the product of the union of the male principle and the female principle, solar fire and the wetness of the earth. This homology in fact underlies most of the rites intended to ensure the fertility of human beings and of the earth, whether the rites of cooking, which are closely dependent on the oppositions which structure the farming year, and are therefore tied to the rhythms of the farming calendar; the rites of renewing the fireplace and stones (*iniyen*), which mark the passage from the wet season to the dry season, or the beginning of the calendar year; and, more generally, all the rites performed within the microcosm of the house. Whenever the women play a part in the specifically agrarian rites, it is again the homology between agricultural fertility and human fertility, the form *par excellence* of all fertility, which underlies their ritual actions and endows them with their magical potency. A considerable number of rites that take place within the house only seem to be domestic rites, since they aim simultaneously to ensure the fertility of the fields and the fertility of the house, which are inextricably linked. For, in order for the field to be full, the house must be full, and woman contributes to the prosperity of the field by dedicating herself, *inter alia*, to accumulating, economizing, and conserving the goods which man has produced and to fixing, as it were, within the house all the good that can enter it. "Man is like the channel, woman like the basin"; one supplies, the other holds and keeps. Man is "the hook on which the baskets are hung"; like the beetle and the bee, he is the provider. What man brings to the house, woman puts away, protects, and saves. It is women who say: "Handle your riches like a log on the fire. There is today, there is tomorrow, there is the grave; God forgives those who have saved, not those who have eaten." And again: "A thrifty woman is worth more than a yoke of oxen ploughing." Just as "the full country" is opposed to "empty space" (*lakhla*), so "the fullness of the house" (*la'mmara ukham*), that is to say, usually the "the old woman" who saves and accumulates, is opposed to "the emptiness of the house" (*lakhla ukham*), usually the daughter-in-law.³⁰ In summer, the door of the house must remain open all day long so that the fertilizing light of the sun can enter, and with it prosperity. A closed door means dearth and sterility: sitting on the threshold – and so blocking it – means closing the passage to happiness and prosperity. To wish someone prosperity, the Kabyles say "May your door remain open" or "May your house be open like a mosque." A rich and generous man is one of whom it is said: "His house is a mosque, it is open to all, rich and poor alike, it is made of wheatcake and couscous, it is full" (*thaʿmmar*); generosity is a sign of prosperity which guarantees prosperity.³¹

Most of the technical and ritual actions which fall to women are oriented by the objective intention of making the house, like *thigedjith* opening its fork to *asalas alemmas*, the receptacle of the prosperity which comes to it from without, the womb which, like the earth, receives the seed the male has put into it; and, conversely, the intention of thwarting all the centrifugal forces which threaten to dispossess the house of the goods entrusted to it. Thus, for example, it is forbidden to give anyone a light from the fire on the day a child or a calf is born, and also on the day when ploughing starts;³² when the threshing has been done, nothing must leave the house and the woman retrieves all the objects that she has lent; the milk produced in the three days following calving must not leave the house; the bride must not cross the threshold before the seventh day after her wedding; a woman who has given birth must not leave the house before the fortieth day; the baby must not go out before the Aïd Seghir; the hand-mill must never be loaned and must not be left empty for fear of bringing famine upon the house; woven cloth must not be taken out before it is finished; like giving embers to light a fire, sweeping, an act of expulsion, is forbidden during the first four days of

30. Applied to a woman, *ʿammar* means to be thrifty and a good housewife; it also means to establish a home and to be full. The opposite of *ʿammar* is the sort of man who is called *ikhla*, extravagant but also sterile and isolated, or *enger*, unmarried and sterile, that is to say, in a sense, wild – incapable, like the jackal, of founding a home.
31. Here too the system of moral values can be seen to derive its fundamental principles from the mythico-ritual system.
32. Conversely, the bringing of new fireplace stones into the house, on inaugural dates, is a filling-up, an input of goodness and prosperity. The forecasts made on these occasions are therefore concerned with prosperity and fertility. If a cockchafer grub is found under one of the stones, there will be a birth in the course of the year; a green plant means a good harvest; ants, a bigger flock; a woodlouse, more cattle.

The Kabyle house

ploughing; when someone dies, the removal of the corpse is "facilitated" so that prosperity is not taken away with it;[33] the first "goings-out", the cow's, for example, four days after calving, or the newborn calf's, are marked by sacrifices.[34] "Emptiness" may result from an act of expulsion; it can also find its way in with certain objects, such as the plough, which must not enter the house between two days' ploughing, or the ploughman's shoes (*arkasen*), which are associated with *lakhla*, empty space; or certain people may bring it in, such as old women, because they are bearers of sterility (*lakhla*) and have caused many houses to be sold or be visited by thieves.

On the other hand, a number of ritual acts aim to ensure the "filling" of the house, such as those which consist of casting the remains of a marriage lamp (whose shape represents sexual union and which plays a part in most fertility rites) into the foundations, after first sacrificing an animal; or of making the bride sit on a leather bag full of grain, on first entering the house. Every first entry into the house is a threat to the fullness of the world inside, a threat which the threshold rites, at once propitiatory and prophylactic, must ward off: a new yoke of oxen is met by the mistress of the house, *thamgharth ukham*, that is, as we have seen, "the fullness of the house", *la'mmara ukham*, who places on the threshold the sheepskin on which the hand-mill stands at other times and which receives the flour (*alamsir*, also called "the door of provisions", *bab errazq*). Most of the rites intended to bring fertility to the stable and, therefore, to the house ("a house without a cow is an empty house"), tend to give magical reinforcement to the structural relationship between milk, the green-blue (*azegzaw*, which is also the raw, *thizegzawth*), grass, springtime – the childhood of the natural world – and human childhood. At the spring equinox, on the "return of *azal*", the young shepherd, who has twofold affinities with the growth of the fields and the cattle on

---

33. To console the bereaved, they are told: "He will leave you the *baraka*", if an adult has died, or "The *baraka* has not gone out of the house", in the case of a baby. The corpse is placed near the door with the head towards the threshold. Water is heated on the stable side and the washing is done near the stable; the embers and ashes of this fire are scattered outside the house; the board used in washing the corpse is left in front of the door for three days; after the burial, three nails are fixed in the door from the Friday to the following Saturday.
34. The cow must step over a knife and some broad beans placed on the threshold; drops of milk are poured on the hearth and threshold.

account of his age and his task, gathers a bouquet to be hung from the lintel of the door and made up of "all that the wind shakes in the countryside" (except for oleander, which is generally used for prophylactic purposes and in the expulsion rites, and scilla, which marks the division between fields). A little bag of herbs, containing cumin, benjamin, and indigo, is buried at the threshold of the stable, with the words: "O green-blue (*azegzaw*), keep the butter from waning!" Freshly picked plants are hung on the butter-churn, and the receptacles used for the milk are rubbed with them.[35] Above all, the new bride's entry is fraught with consequences for the fertility and plenitude of the house: while she is still seated on the mule which has carried her from her father's house, she is presented with water, grains of wheat, figs, nuts, cooked eggs, or fritters, all of which (whatever the local variants) are things associated with the fertility of woman and of the land; she throws them towards the house, thus ensuring that she is preceded by the fertility and plenitude she must bring to the house.[36] She crosses the threshold carried on the back of one of her husband's kinsmen or sometimes, according to Maunier, on the back of a Negro, but never, in any case, on her husband's back; for the person who carries her interposes himself, intercepting the malignant forces which might otherwise affect her fertility and of which the threshold, the meeting point between two opposed worlds, is the site. A woman must never sit near the threshold holding her child; and a young child and a bride should not tread it too often. Thus, woman, through whom fertility comes to the house, makes her own contribution to the fertility of the fields: consigned to the world of the inside, she also acts on the outside by ensuring plenitude for the inside and, in her role as guardian of the threshold, by supervising those unrequited exchanges which only the logic of magic can conceive, through which each part of the universe expects to receive from the other nothing but fullness while giving it only emptiness.[37]

35. In some places when a young shepherd hears the first cuckoo he picks up a stone and puts it on his head; this stone is then put into the vessel used to receive the milk. Elsewhere the milk may be drawn through the handle-ring of a pickaxe or a pinch of earth may be thrown into the container.
36. She may also be sprinkled with water or given water and milk to drink.
37. Various objects are hung in the doorway; they have in common the fact that they manifest the dual function of the threshold, a selective barrier whose purpose is to keep

But one or the other of the two systems of oppositions which define the house, either in its internal organization or in its relationship with the external world, is brought to the forefront depending on whether the house is considered from the male or the female point of view. Whereas for the man the house is not so much a place he goes into as a place he comes out of, the woman is bound to give the opposite importance and meaning to these two movements and to the different definitions of the house which they imply, since, for her, movement outwards consists above all in acts of expulsion, and movement inwards, that is, from the threshold towards the hearth, is her proper concern. The significance of movement outwards is never more clearly seen than in the rite performed by a mother, seven days after giving birth, "in order that her son may be valorous": striding across the threshold, she sets her right foot upon the carding comb and simulates a fight with the first boy she meets. Going out is the essentially male movement, which leads towards other men and also towards the dangers and trials which must be *confronted* with the determination of a man as prickly, in matters of honour, as the spikes of the carding comb.[38] Going out or, more exactly, opening (*fataḥ*) is the equivalent of "being in the morning" (*ṣebaḥ*). A self-respecting man must leave the house at daybreak; morning is the day of the daytime and leaving the house in the morning is a birth. Hence the importance of the things encountered, which are a portent for the whole day, so that in the event of an undesirable encounter (a smith, a woman carrying an empty leather bag, shouts or a quarrel, a deformed being), it is better to go back and "remake one's morning" or one's "going out".

It is now clear why it is so important which way the house faces. The front of the main house, the one which shelters the head of the family and which contains a stable, almost always faces east, and the main door – as opposed to the low, narrow door, reserved for the women, which leads to the garden – is commonly called the east door (*thabburth thacherqith*), or else the street door, the upper

out emptiness and evil while letting in fullness and goodness and predisposing towards fertility and prosperity everything which crosses the threshold towards the outside world.

38. A newborn girl is wrapped in the softness of a silk scarf; a boy is swathed in the dry, rough bindings that are used to tie sheaves.

door, or the great door.[39] Given the siting of the villages and the lower position of the stable, the upper part of the house, with the fireplace, is in the north, the stable in the south, and the weaving-loom wall in the west. It follows from this that the movement by which one approaches the house to enter it is oriented from east to west, in opposition to the movement made when coming out, in accordance with the orientation *par excellence*, towards the east, that is, towards the high, the bright, the good, and the prosperous: the ploughman turns his oxen to face the east when he harnesses and unharnesses them and he starts ploughing from west to east; likewise, the harvesters work facing *elqibla* and the sacrificial ox is slain facing eastward. Countless actions are performed in accordance with the cardinal orientation; they include all the actions of importance, that is, all those involving the fertility and prosperity of the group.[40] It is sufficient to recall that the verb *qabel* means not only to face up to, to confront with honour and receive worthily, but also to face the east (*elqibla*) and the future (*qabel*).

If we now go back to the internal organization of the house, we can see that its orientation is exactly the reverse of that of external space, as if it had been obtained by a semi-rotation around the axis of the front wall or the threshold. The weaving-loom wall, which a person entering immediately faces on crossing the threshold, and which is lit directly by the morning sun, is the light of the inside (just as woman is the lamp of the inside), that is, the east of the inside, symmetrical to the external east, from which it draws its borrowed light.[41] The dark, inside face of the front wall represents

39. It goes without saying that the opposite arrangement (as in a mirror image of the diagram on p. 152) is possible, though rare. It is explicitly said that all that comes from the west brings misfortune, and a door facing that direction can only receive darkness and sterility. In fact, if the inversion of the "ideal" ground-plan is rare, this is mainly because when secondary houses are set at right angles around the courtyard, they are often simply lodging rooms, without kitchen or table, and because the courtyard is often closed off, on the side opposite the front of the main house, by the back of the neighbouring house, which itself faces east.

40. The two *ṣufs*, political and martial factions which are mobilized as soon as any incident occurred (and which maintained variable relations with the kinship-based social units, ranging from superimposition to complete separation) were named *ṣuf* of the upper part (*ufella*) and *ṣuf* of the lower (*buadda*), or *ṣuf* of the right (*ayafus*) and *ṣuf* of the left (*azelmadh*), or *ṣuf* of the east (*acherqi*) and *ṣuf* of the west (*aghurbi*). The last pair of terms was less common but was kept to designate the two sides in the ritual games (from which the traditional battles between the *ṣufs* derived their logic); it still survives nowadays in the language of children's games.

41. As we have seen, the master of the house receives (*qabel*) his guests on the weaving-loom side, the noble part of the house.

The Kabyle house

the west of the house, the place of sleep, which one leaves behind one as one moves towards the *kanun*; the door corresponds symbolically to the "door of the year", the opening of the wet season and the farming year. Likewise, the two gable walls, the stable wall and the fireplace wall, receive two opposing meanings depending on which of their sides is being considered: to the external north corresponds the south (and summer) of the inside, that is, the part of the house which is in front of and to the right of a person who enters facing the loom; to the external south corresponds the internal north (and winter), that is, the stable, which is behind and to the left of someone going from the door towards the fire.[42] The division of the house into a dark part (the west and north sides) and a bright part (the east and south sides) corresponds to the division of the year into a wet season and a dry season. In short, to each external face of the wall (*essur*) corresponds a region of the internal space (which the Kabyles refer to as *tharkunt*, which means, roughly, a side) which possesses a symmetrical but opposite meaning in the system of internal oppositions. Each of the two spaces can thus be defined as the class of movements undergoing the same displacement, i.e. a semi-rotation, with respect to the other, with the threshold constituting the axis of rotation.[43] The importance and symbolic value given to the threshold within the system cannot be fully understood unless it is seen that it owes its function as a magical boundary to the fact that it is the site of a logical inversion and that, as the necessary meeting point and the locus of passages between the two spaces that are defined in terms of body movements and socially qualified crossings,[44] it is logically the place where the world is reversed.[45]

Thus, each of the two universes has its own east, and the two

---

42. The four cardinal points and the four seasons must therefore be added to the series of oppositions and homologies set out above (and it can be demonstrated that these significations belong to and are adequate to the mythico-ritual system as a whole):
...culture: nature:: east: west:: south: north:: spring: autumn:: summer: winter.
43. For an analysis of the theoretical implications of the fact that the transformational rules which permit the passage from one space to the other can be related back to movements of the body, see Bourdieu, *Outline of a Theory of Practice*, pp. 116–19.
44. In certain regions of Kabylia, the young bride, and a boy circumcised at the time of the same celebration, must cross paths on the threshold.
45. This explains why the threshold is directly or indirectly associated with the rites intended to bring about a reversal of the course of events by carrying out a reversal of the basic oppositions: the rites to obtain rain or fine weather, for instance, or those performed on the threshold at the turning points of the year (e.g. the night before *ennayer*, the first day of the solar year, when charms are buried at the threshold).

152   Algeria 1960

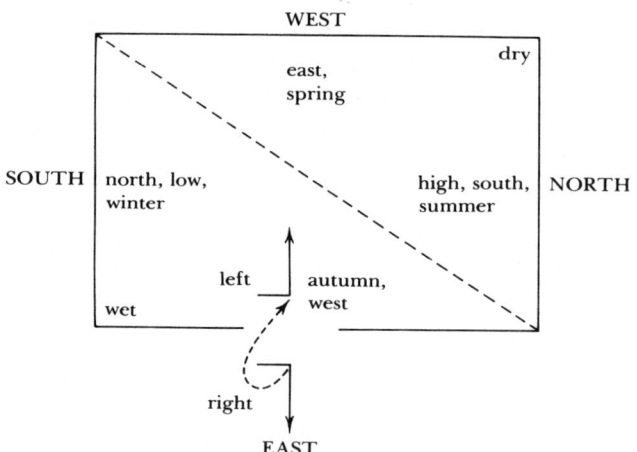

Fig. 2. The dual space orientation of the house

movements most fraught with magical significance and consequences – displacement from the threshold to the hearth, which should bring fullness and is performed or ritually controlled by woman, and displacement from the threshold to the outside world, which, by virtue of its inaugural value, contains all that the future will bring, especially the future of the farming work – can each be carried out in accordance with the beneficent orientation, that is, from west to east.[46] The dual space orientation of the house means that one is able both to go in and go out on the right foot, literally and figuratively, with the magical advantage attached to this observance, without there ever being a break in the relation linking the right to the high, the bright, and the good. The semi-rotation of space around the threshold thus ensures, as it were, the maximizing of magical profit, since both centripetal movement and centrifugal movement are performed in a space so organized that one enters it facing the light and also comes out of it facing the light.[47]

46. The correspondence between the four corners of the house and the four cardinal points is expressed clearly in certain propitiatory rites observed in the Aurès: when the fireplace is renewed, on the new year's day, the Chaouïa woman cooks some fritters, divides the first one cooked into four pieces, and throws them in the direction of the four corners of the house. She does the same thing with the ritual dish on the first day of spring (see M. Gaudry, *La femme chaouïa de l'Aurès* (Paris: L. Geuthner, Librairie Orientaliste, 1928, pp. 58–9).
47. I shall endeavour to show elsewhere that the same structure is to be found in the temporal order. But to indicate that this is doubtless an instance of a very general form of magical thought, one further, very similar, example will suffice: the Arabs of the

The Kabyle house

The two symmetrical and opposite spaces are not interchangeable but hierarchized; the inner space is but the inverted image or mirror reflection of male space.[48] It is no accident that only the direction the door faces is explicitly prescribed, the internal organization of space never being consciously perceived as such – still less deliberately planned – by those who inhabit it.[49] The orientation of the house is fundamentally defined from outside, from the standpoint of men, and, so to speak, by men and for men, as the place men come out of. "A house prospers through woman; its outside is beautiful through man." The house is an empire within an empire, but one which always remains subordinate because, even when it exhibits all the properties and all the relations which define the archetypal world, it remains an inverted reflection, a world in reverse.[50] "Man is the lamp of the outside, woman the lamp of the inside." One must not be misled by the appearance of symmetry: the lamp of day is only apparently defined in relation to the lamp of night. In fact the nocturnal light, the female male, remains subordinate to the diurnal light, the lamp of day, that is, to the day of the daytime. "Man trusts in God, woman looks to man for everything." "Woman", it is also said, "is twisted like a sickle"; and so even the straightest of these warped natures is only ever straightened up. Once married, woman also finds her east, within the house of man, but her east is only the inversion of a west; for "the maiden is the west". The supremacy given to movement outwards, in which man affirms his manliness by turning his back on the house in order to face other men, choosing the way of the east of the world, is only one form of the categorical refusal of nature, the inevitable origin of the movement away from it.

   Maghreb considered it a good sign, Ben Cheneb relates, for a house to have its right front foot and its left rear foot white in colour; the master of such a horse cannot fail to be happy, since he mounts towards white and also dismounts towards white (Arab horsemen mount on the right and dismount on the left) (see Ben Cheneb, *Proverbes d'Alger et du Maghreb* (Paris: Leroux, 1905–7), vol. 3, p. 312).
48. Mirrors play an important part in inversion rites, particularly those to obtain fine weather.
49. This explains why it has escaped the notice of even the most attentive observers.
50. In the internal space too, the two opposed parts are hierarchized. The following saying is yet another index of this: "A house full of men is better than a house full of chattels [*el mal*]", i.e. cattle.

Index

accountancy, 3, 11, 17, 43, 46, 55
"acculturation", 1, 30
accumulation, 11, 19
aid, mutual (*thiwizi*), 13, 14, 20, 36, 37, 78
alienation, 61
amahbul, 95–6, 101
anthropologist, 2, 16, 30, 115–16
anthropology: cultural, 1; economics and, 6; structural, 22
arbitrariness, 3–4, 29, 35, 62
aspirations, 28, 50–4, 61, 62, 67, 70–2
assembly, 120n, 129, 141, 142
awareness, *see* consciousness

barter, 11–12
beam, main, 103, 139–41
behaviour, *see* conduct
Bernard, A., 11
Berque, A., 11
bilingualism, 38, 73–4
body, 125, 151–2
borrowing, 14, 18, 21, 66; cultural, 30; *see also* aid, credit, loan
budget, 45, 47, 55, 80, 82, 85, 88; *see also* family, rent

calculability, 6–7, 21, 43–4, 48, 68, 73; threshold of, 54
calculation, 3–4, 8–12, 15–22, 42–8, 50, 52, 55, 66, 68, 72–4, 78, 82, 88n, 90; *see also* future
calendar, agrarian, 27–8, 145; *see also* cycle, time
capital, 21–2, 55; symbolic, 22–3, 116ff, 130–2; *see also* accumulation, economy
capitalism, 3–4, 25–6, 68
Cavaillès, J., 8
challenge, 96, 99–102, 106–7
change: culture, 1, 2n, 30, 64–5; exogenous, 3; social, 30, 61, 64–5
Chomsky, N., 95

city, *see* towns
civil servants, 35, 40, 45n, 71, 75n, 76; *see also* petty bourgeois
class, 2, 49, 52–3, 64, 90–3
clerical workers, 4, 34, 35, 36, 66, 71, 75n; *see also* civil servants, petty bourgeois
cohabitation (of undivided family), 46–7, 69, 77, 78–9; *see also* housing, rent
colonial system, 3, 30, 58, 62, 65
colonization, 3, 13, 14, 62, 65, 73n
conduct, 21, 40, 43, 56, 60, 68–9, 71–2, 88n; disorganization of, 48–9, 62, 67; economic, 1, 4, 7, 43–4, 46, 50, 65, 92; of foresight, 9; harmonization of, 41; of honour, 95–132; new, 44; objective future as basis of, 92; ostentatious, 19; rationalization of, 46, 54, 74; restructuring of, 72, 74–5; resurgence of traditional, 68
consciousness: class, 2, 56, 61, 70, 92–4; economic, 6; political, 39; revolutionary, 50, 62, 72; temporal, 7, 16, *and see* time; of unemployment, 41, 50, 56–7, 62; *see also* discourse, plan
contract, 3, 13–14, 18, 21–2
counting forbidden, 15; *see also* accountancy, calculation
crafts, 33, 36, 47, 55–6
craftsmen, 36, 38, 47, 48, 51n, 71, 76, 78, 84
credit, 13–14, 41, 55, 79; bank, 88n, 90; based on confidence, 69, 71, 78; *see also* borrowing, deadline, usury
culture, *see* nature, tradition
customary law, 13, 129–30
cycle: agrarian, 10, 29, 33; cosmic, 23; life-cycle, 29, 138; of production and reproduction, 10; of work, 24; *see also* calendar, future, reproduction, time

deadline (for payment): fixed, 80–1, 88; not fixed, 14, 21–2; *see also* credit, loan

156 Index

Desparmet, J., 15
dialectic of challenge and riposte, 99ff, 114n, 118; *see also* challenge, exchange
discourse, 56–8, 69; *see also* bilingualism, language
discrepancy: between dispositions and structures, 6; between habitus and structures, vii, 4; between subjective certainty and objective truth, 21, 22n
dispositions: adaptation of, 5; customary, 4; economic, vii, 2–5, 16, 47, 48, 50n, 54, 64, 71, 75, 85, 90, 92; logic of acquired, 32; to revolt, viii; system of, 2, 5, 6, 16, 30, 50n, 54, 58, 64, 72, 90–2; *see also* habitus, time
door, 146, 149–50; *see also* threshold
Durkheim, E., 129

economics and anthropology, 6
economy: agrarian, 10; capitalist, vii, 6–7, 10, 16, 45, 48, 65; cash, 2, 4, 9, 17, 45, 78; colonial, 65; domestic, 6, 47, 54, 75n, 81, 85; in itself, 23; modern, 9n, 32, 48, 72–3; of poverty, 68–9, 79; pre-capitalist, vii, 6–8, 13, 16–17, 25, 45, 65; rational, 2, 65
education, 4, 7, 30, 48, 52, 74, 85, 91, 123, 126–7
elbahadla, 98–9, 101, 109
emancipation, 47–8
embourgeoisement, 37, 63, 91
emigration, *see* towns
employment, 33–40, 42, 47, 52, 54, 57, 61, 62, 66–9, 70–1, 88n; full, 57; *see also* income, labour, unemployment, wages, women
ethic(s), 9, 14, 18–19, 26–8; female, 123–4; Protestant, 25–6; *see also* honour
ethnocentrism, 5, 16, 17n, 110n
ethos, 7, 9, 16–18, 24, 65; of honour, 128ff; pre-capitalist, 28, 41
Europeans, 48, 59, 72, 79, 84n, 86–7; as colonists, 10, 60
exchange: and challenge, 105–10, 113–17; of gifts, 19, 21–3, 106–9; in kind, and commercial, 11; meal as, 20; monetary, 10–12; ritual, 18, 91n; of services, 25; of women, 127; *see also* loan, money
expectations, 27, 28, 52
expenditure, 46, 90; on housing, 76–85, 88, 90; joint, and several wages, 69, 76–7; *see also* housing, income, rent, wages

facing up to (*qabel*), 106n, 113, 123, 128, 136, 141, 149–50
faction (*ṣuf*), 21, 102, 150n
family, 17, 19–20, 22, 24–5, 35–6, 44–9, 52, 54–5, 56n, 67, 69, 75–9, 82, 84–5, 87–8, 89–90; *see also* aid, solidarity
Fanon, F., 62
fatalism, 60, 62, 67, 92
female/male, 120–7, 137–8, 139, 140, 142–3, 145; female–female and male–female, 142–3; *see also* oppositions
fertility, 9, 17, 72–3, 74, 76n, 138–40, 145ff
forecasting, 4, 8, 11–12, 17, 28, 62, 66, 72–4, 82; *see also* foresight, predictability
foreman, 35, 39, 58
foresight, 8, 10, 49, 68, 69
future, 8, 14–16, 26–7, 28, 50–3, 62, 68–70, 72–3, 74, 85, 128; abstract, 10, 13; calculated, 29, 68; children's, 51–4; class, 64; collective, viii, 2, 64; dispositions towards, 7; as field of possibles, 8, 15, 28, 50; and money, 11–12; objective, vii–viii, 2, 64, 92; *see also* calculation, hopes, needs, possibles, probabilities, time

generosity, 19, 97, 114, 146
Genevoix, H., 134n, 136n
gift, *see* exchange
guarantee, 10, 13, 14, 71

Habakkuk, H. J., 17
habitus, vii, 2, 4, 32, 54, 65, 92, 116, 132n; *see also* dispositions
Hanoteau, A., 13n
hearth, 82, 84, 134, 144, 145, 146
hoarding, *see* reserves
homo economicus, 2, 6
honour, 9, 14, 18–19, 22, 45, 49, 74; (*ḥurma*), 101, 102, 117–20, 136–42, 144n; man of, 101–2, 112–15, 119, 128; (*nif*), 101, 102–6, 110–21, 136, 140; (*sar*), 118–19
hopes, 11, 16, 52–3, 62, 69, 72
house, Kabyle, 122–5, 133–53; and assembly, 141, 142; bipartite, 133–8, 143–4, 150–1, 153n; building of, and rites, 19, 138; and marriage, 139–40; orientation, 149–53; and tomb, 136n, 138n; for woman, 136n, 140–1, 149; and world, 140–3
housing, modern, 72–91; shortage, 46, 49
Hume, D., 1
ḥurma, see under honour

illiteracy, 34–5, 55; *see also* education, sub-proletarians
imaginary, the, 7, 10, 11, 53
income, 9, 13, 41–3, 44–7, 52–4, 57, 61–2, 68, 69, 71, 72–3, 74, 75–9, 88, 90; estimated and real, 51; maximizing, 71; monetary, 33, 38, 47, 48; several, *see*

Index

wages; *see also* expenditure, family, needs, rent, wages
innovation, 19, 27
inside/outside, *see* oppositions

job, *see* employment, labour, unemployment
Jourdan, A., 11

Kabyles, 12, 15, 21, 27, 33, 49, 57
Kabylia, 19, 45, 57; villages, 11, 19, 87, 122; *see also* house
kanun, *see* hearth
khammes, 9, 11, 25, 36n, 65, 97–8
kind: compensation in, 18, 20; exchanges in, 11; product in, 42

labour, 10, 17, 23–7, 33, 40–4, 51–7, 70–1, 79; collective, 19–20; division of, between sexes, 89, 91, 126, 137–8; and keeping busy, 25, 33, 40, 41–3, 71; and pains, 23, 41–2; productive and unproductive, 25–6; as social function, 25, 40–3, 57; and transformation of world, 29; *see also* employment, income, unemployment
labourers, unskilled, 34–6, 37–9, 53, 61, 64, 66, 70, 75n, 76, 78, 81, 85n; *see also* sub-proletarians
Lacroix, N., 11
land, 21–2, 23–4; dispossession of, 13, 14; ownership of, 17
language, 38, 66, 73–4; *see also* discourse
Laoust, E., 126n, 134n, 137n
Lerner, D., 31–2
Lévi-Strauss, C., 22n
loan, 11, 13, 21; *see also* aid, borrowing, credit, deadline
loom, 135–7, 144, 150
Lukács, G., 23

magic, 121, 124, 148, 152
marabouts, 98, 103, 107
Marcy, G., 106
marginal utility, theory of, 5
marginalism, neo-, vii
Marx, K., 17
Maunier, R., 20n, 134n, 139, 144, 148
misrecognition, 23, 46, 130
mobility, social, 51–3; *see also* future, plan
model, 2, 22, 116
modernity, 31; threshold of, 91
"modernization" theory, 31–2
modesty, 112–13, 122–6; *see also* nakedness
money, 10–13, 17, 20–1, 43, 46, 96–7; *see also* credit, exchange, income, loan

Montesquieu, 130
myth, 26–7; *see also* oppositions, rites

nakedness, 96n, 125n
nature: and culture, 136, 140, 144, 153; and human work, 23, 26; struggle against, 29; *see also* peasants
needs, 11–12, 44, 50–1, 52, 67, 68, 71–3, 75, 87, 90; *see also* aspirations
Negro, 102, 148
Nietzsche, F., 32–3
nif, *see under* honour

objectivism, vii, 92
observer, *see* anthropologist
oppositions, mythico-ritual, 27, 120–9, 135–44

peasants, 8–10, 13, 14, 16, 21, 23–8, 33, 36, 41, 44, 49, 55, 62, 68, 69–70, 73n
petty bourgeois, 40, 59, 91; *see also* clerical workers
piston, *see* "string-pulling"
plan, 8–10, 49, 50–1, 59, 62, 68–9
possibles, 8, 14–15, 16, 29, 44, 50–1; *see also* calculation, future, plan
potentialities, objective, 14, 64, 92; *see also* probabilities
pre-capitalist, *see* economy, ethos
predictability, 7, 27, 68–9, 74; *see also* calculability
probabilities, objective, vii, 92
profitability, 9, 40–1, 55; *see also* calculation, labour
project, viii, 10, 29, 50–1, 53, 62, 94
proletariat, viii, 62, 69–70, 71–2, 91

qabel, *see* facing up to
Qaddoûr ben Klîfa, 15
quasi-systematization, affective, 58–60, 93

rationalization, 1, 4–7, 46, 54, 55, 64–6, 68; *see also* calculation, conduct
realism, 72, 73–4
religion, 60, 62, 69–70
rent, 76–81, 83–6, 88n
reproduction, 10, 17, 130, 132n
reserve army, industrial, 33–4
reserves, 8–9, 11, 12, 33
revolutionary action, 72
revolutionary *cogito*, 61
revolutionary consciousness, 50, 62, 72
revolutionary force, 62
revolutionary millenarianism, 70
revolutionary war, 56n
rifle, 105, 120, 136

158   Index

rites, 9, 19–20, 23–4, 27–8, 104–5, 115–16, 136–8, 146–8; and strategy, 115–16
ritualization, 103–4

sacred (*haram*), 117ff
sar, see under honour
saving, vii, 68, 74
Sayad, A., 2n, 33n
secret, 119–28, 138, 141, 142
security, 8, 35, 49, 54, 62, 65, 66, 70–1, 74
sexual relations, 125, 136, 138–9
shame, 96, 113–14, 137
shanty town, 49, 68–9, 75n, 76–9, 80–3, 86, 88, 91, 93n
"shanty townization", 87
shopkeepers, *see* traders
Simiand, F., 11–12
sociology, 12, 30–1
solidarity, 13, 20, 33, 35, 42, 45, 63, 78, 86n, 88
Sombart, W., 3–4
spending, *see* expenditure
status, 42, 51, 90
stereotype, 58
stereotyping, 26, 49, 116
strategy, 105, 116, 132n; economic, 65; reproduction, 132n
"string-pulling", 59–61
structure, vii, 4–5, 132n
subjectivism, 5
sub-proletarians, viii, 35, 36–8, 48–9, 50–3, 60–3, 65–70, 72, 91, 93
target-shooting, 104–5
technical, the, and the ritual, 23, 135
thiwizi, see aid
threshold, 122n, 148–53; *see also* calculability, modernity

time, 2, 6–7, 10, 11, 13, 14–15, 16, 17, 18, 22, 26–9, 55, 66, 67, 115–16
time-lag, 22, 115–16
towns, 33, 36n, 41, 42, 44, 45, 47, 55–6, 62, 66, 69–70, 77n, 78, 81, 87; emigration to, 13, 17n, 36n, 51n, 57, 70; size of, 77n
traders, 36, 44, 46, 52n, 55–6, 64, 66, 71n, 75n, 76, 78, 84n; itinerant, 40–1, 87
tradition, 4, 9, 11, 19, 23n, 28–9, 35, 49, 57, 65–6, 68, 69–70, 74, 82, 89–90
traditionalism, 26–7, 28–9, 41–2, 49, 68, 73, 87

undivided land ownership, 17, 45, 49, 130; breakup of, 13, 46, 49; and undivided honour, 110, 111n
unemployment, 33–5, 38–42, 50, 56–8, 59, 64, 65–70, 71; and disorganization, 66–7; *see also under* consciousness
urban world, *see* towns
usury, 13, 55

vengeance (*thamgart*), 102, 107–8, 110–11; and cash compensation, 118
villages, 11, 19–20, 28, 82, 87, 144
Violette, M., 13

wages, 13, 20, 37–8, 44–5, 47, 67, 71–2, 77–82; several, 69, 77–9, 80, 88; *see also* expenditure, income
Weber, M., 3, 5, 25–6
work, *see* employment, income, labour, wages, women
women, 9, 12, 47; living space, 88–9, 122–3, 138, 140–2; work, 38, 47, 54, 67, 79; *see also* female/male; labour, division of